Celebrating Life with Yoga

Celebrating Life with Yoga

Ajay Bhardwaj

DK PRINTWORLD
Publishers of Indian Traditions

Cataloging in Publication Data – DK
[Courtesy: D.K. Agencies (P) Ltd. <docinfo@dkagencies.com>]

Bharadwaj, Ajay, 1972- **author.**
Celebrating life with yoga / Ajay Bhardwaj.
page cm
Includes bibliographical references and index.
ISBN 9788124608951

1. Yoga. 2. Hatha yoga. I. Title.

LCC BL1238.52.B43 2018 | DDC 294.5436 23

ISBN: 978-81-246-0895-1
First published in India in 2019

Printed and published by:
D.K. Printworld (P) Ltd.
Regd. Office: "Vedaśrī", F-395, Sudarshan Park
(Metro Station: ESI Hospital),
New Delhi - 110015
Phones: (011) 2545 3975, 2546 6019
e-mail: indology@dkprintworld.com
Website: www.dkprintworld.com

Preface

TODAY a large number of people suffer from various physical and mental ailments, and they are mainly lifestyle related. There is no permanent cure for many a disease like diabetes and blood pressure. One has to undergo lifelong treatment to negate the challenges of such diseases. Ages ago, our saints and sages knew the importance and method of remaining healthy to lead a fulfilling life. Their philosophy reflects well in the saying: *sharir madhyam khalu dharma sadhanam*, meaning that the body is the primary medium for performing our personal and social functions.

Emphasizing the importance of human life, Goswami Tulsidas in his *Ramacharitmanas* has aptly remarked: *bade bhagya manush tan pava*, implying that this human body has been achieved by great destiny and effort. In fact, nothing is so beautiful and fulfilling as the human life. Because an individual can achieve the supreme goal of his life, i.e. enlightenment, and devote himself to serve the entire humanity. It is equally true that only a cultured and civilized individual can be the basis of a cultured and civilized society, just as only an enlightened being can show light to others. The ancient saints, seers and *yogi*s, although having no material comforts, would lead a blissful life. Why? Because they had a holistic lifestyle. They adopted *yoga* as a spiritual means, a lifestyle and as the philosophy of life.

Since *yoga*-centred spirituality paves the way for the physical, mental and spiritual well-being of an individual, through such individuals the society gets transformed into a healthy, harmonious, prosperous, peaceful and blissful entity. All the great *yogi*s had specified the importance of applying the yogic and spiritual lifestyle for the overall benefit of the society. They validated the adoration of life deity through spiritual lifestyle on the one hand and the social fellowship and unification through the experiment of the collective *sadhana* on the other. While the yogic lifestyle provides one the inner vision of peace and perfection in every action, it also provides him the spiritual vision to see the entire creation as the manifestation of his very soul. He begins to see all beings in himself and himself in all beings.

Today people are flocking to *yoga* for their well-being. Several researches on *yoga* have shown that it is successful in curing several physical and mental disorders. Today people have begun to realize, validate and propagate that *yoga* can mitigate many health issues what medicines and other health-care products can't. This has led to the widespread popularity of *yoga* even among the youth and celebrities as they want to gain and maintain their physical charm and fitness. No doubt, in recent years, people's interest in *yoga* has increased manifold but it is equally true that people aren't aware of the true form and purpose of *yoga*. Some *asanas* and *kriyas*, which they consider *yoga*, are merely physical exercises, and they reflect only the external aspect of *yoga*. It is this aspect of *yoga* that has gained wide acceptance, first in the Western countries and later in India.

A number of *yoga* clubs have mushroomed in India and abroad where the so-called *yoga gurus* are projecting *yoga* merely as a means of physical exercises rather than an extraordinary science of self-development and self-realization. Although *yoga* is helpful in gaining physical well-being, it is not the ultimate goal of *yoga*. Self-realization is its ultimate goal. *Yoga* in fact begins with the purity of mind. That is why Maharshi Patanjali recommends *yama* and *niyama* in his *ashtanga-yoga*. Thus there is the dire need to present the true form and purpose of *yoga* before the common masses; otherwise they would remain unaware of the reality about it and will remain confused. Media can play a major role in educating the masses on the ultimate purpose of *yoga*, in addition to its effects on physical well-being. We must practise *yoga* in our daily life for physical, mental and spiritual well-being. Thus by following the royal path of *yoga* we can celebrate every moment, leading a pious, prosperous, peaceful and blissful life.

Coming to the chapter scheme, Chapter 1 "Yoga: Meaning and Concept" details the meaning, definitions and concept of *yoga* as per the ancient and modern yogic texts and *yogis*. Chapter 2 "History and Traditions of Yoga" deliberates on the history and different traditions of *yoga*.

Chapter 3 "Different Paths of Yoga" discusses *raja-yoga*, *hatha-yoga*, *mantra-yoga*, *laya-yoga*, *jnana-yoga*, *karma-yoga* and *bhakti-yoga*. Chapter 4 "Importance and Applications of Yoga" details the role and importance of *yoga* in our day-to-day life for physical, mental and spiritual well-being.

Chapter 5 "Practice of Yoga" presents important suggestions and guidance in persuing the practice of *yoga*.

While writing this book, I have tried to consult and assimilate all the aspects of *yoga* and spirituality and therefore tried to illustrate various points with latest examples from newspapers, magazines, research journals and other sources. The views of *yoga* experts, scholars and journalists, who have been active in academic and professional fields, are incorporated to enrich the contents. I hope, it will help in propagating the message of *yoga* in its true form and spirit, and will create awareness among people about *yoga* for their well-being and enlightenment.

Written in a simple language, this book, I hope, would be useful to *yoga* aspirants, *yoga* teachers and common man alike. It is my belief that it would be a step forward in the society understanding *yoga* better.

Suggestions for improvement are welcome and such inputs, I am sure, will add value to the forthcoming editions.

Ajay Bhardwaj
<dsvvajay@gmail.com>

Acknowledgements

My obeisance to Goddess Sarasvati and Lord Ganesh, the originators of letters and their meaning, of poetic sentiments and metres, for their blessings.

A journey is easier when we travel together. This book is a result of five years of work in which I was accompanied and escorted by many people. It is now a pleasant feeling to express my gratitude to all of them. There is a strong temptation to acknowledge those who have played a major role in shaping up this work by a personal note of gratitude.

First of all, I seek the blessings of Lord Shiva, the all wise and eternal *guru*, through whom even the crescent moon, though crooked in shape, is universally honoured. Equal is my devotion to Goddess Parvati. Also is my adulation to the great masters Sri Ramakrishna Paramahansa, Swami Vivekananda, Maharshi Aurobindo, Ramana Maharshi, Yugrishi Shriram Sharma Acharya, and the holy mothers Sri Sharda Mani, Sri Maa and Bhagwati Devi Sharma.

I adore the holy Jiji Shailbala Pandya and Honourable Dr Pranav Pandya, the spiritual head of All World Gayatri Pariwar, and the Chancellor of Dev Sanskriti Vishvavidyalaya, Shantikunj, Haridwar who, like my preceptors and parents, have always been very supportive with their parental care and guidance. I convey my thanks to Dr Chinmay Pandya, Pro-Vice-Chancellor, Dev Sanskriti Vishvavidyalaya, Haridwar, who, like my elder brother, encouraged me in accomplishing this work.

I bow in respect to the lotus feet of Shri Jitendra Tiwari, for his keen interest and constant encouragement in executing this project.

My homage to the lotus feet of my mother, late Shanti Devi, and my father late Sri Arjun Sharma who were always my source of inspiration. Words cannot articulate feelings of gratitude to my wife, Nutan Bhardwaj and my daughter, Nivedita for their constant support and cooperation. Without their keen interest and assistance, this work would not have found fruition.

I am extremely grateful to Dr Kamakhya Kumar, HoD of Yoga, Uttarakhand Sanskrit Vishvavidyalaya, Haridwar; Shri Balrup Sharma, Shantikunj, Haridwar; Dr Govind Singh, Examination Controller, Uttarakhand Open University, Haldwani; Shri Sudeep Thakur, Associate Editor, *Amar Ujala*, New Delhi and Sri Kalol Chakravarti, *Amar Ujala*, New Delhi for providing me motivation and support.

Above all, I would like to thank the Almighty, Omnipotent and Omnipresent God for providing me strength and courage to accomplish this task well in time.

Ajay Bhardwaj

Contents

1

Yoga : Meaning and Concept

THE word *yoga* is derived from the Sanskrit root *yuj*, which means to yoke or to unite. In later times, however, another technical meaning came to be associated with the term, and this is derived from *yujir samadhau*, which means "contemplation" or "absorption".[1]

The first use of the root of *yoga* is found in hymn V.81.1 of *Rigveda* where it has been interpreted as "yoke" or "union":

> Men illumined yoke their mind and they yoke their thoughts to him who is illumination and largeness and clear perceiving. Knowing all phenomena he orders, sole, the energies of sacrifice. Vast is the affirmation in all things of Savitri, the Divine Creator.

Kathopanishad II.3.10-11 states:

> The supreme path begins when the five senses and the mind are stilled and when the intellect is silent. This tranquillity of the senses is *yoga*.

Agni Purana 183.1.3 states:

> When the light of knowledge dawns on *chitta*, it becomes concentrated and becomes like Brahma Himself; and thus occurs the communion of the individual soul with the supreme soul. Such a concentrated state of *chitta* is called *yoga*.

Gita defines *yoga* thus:

i. *Yoga* is equanimity in success and failure (II.48).

ii. *Yoga* is excellence in action (II.50).

---

[1] http://en.wikipedia.org/yoga_sutra

iii. *Yoga* is the dissociation of the association with suffering (VI. 23).

Maharshi Patanjali in his *Yogasutra* 1.2 says:

> *Yoga* is the inhibition (*nirodha*) of the modifications (*vritti*) of the mind.

Yoga-Vasishtha VI.13.3 defines *yoga*:

> as a device by which one goes across the ocean of suffering; i.e. *yoga* is a means of living the life of a *jivanmukta* (liberated soul) which is the ultimate end of human life.

Hatha-Yoga Pradipika (4.7) states:

> The *yoga* is a state of ecstasy or trance.

Swami Vivekananda says:

> *Yoga* is restraining the mind stuff (*chitta*) from taking various forms (*vrittis*). As the reflection of the moon on the sea is broken or blurred by the waves, so is the reflection of the *atman*, the true self, broken by the mental waves. Only when the sea is stilled to mirror like calmness can the reflection of the moon be seen, and only when the mind stuff, the *chitta*, is controlled to absolute calmness, is the self to be recognized.[2]

He further says:

> *Yoga* is a science which teaches how to awaken our latent powers and hasten the process of human evolution. It is restraining the mind stuff from taking different forms.[3]

Maharshi Aurobindo says:

> *Yoga* is a methodological effort towards self-perfection by development of potentialities latent within the individual.[4]

---

[2] Vivekananda, 2000, *Six Lessons on Raja-Yoga*, p. 7.

[3] Ibid.

[4] www.hindustanwisdom.in of/yoga and hindu philosophy.htm (17 July 2008).

Ramana Maharshi says:

> Yoga is the process of self-inquiry and knowing oneself: who am I?[5]

Yugrishi Shriram Sharma Acharya says:

> The general meaning of the word *yoga* is to unite. In spiritual language, the communion of the individual soul with the supreme soul is called *yoga* and the activities which are adopted to begin this is called *sadhana* (spiritual disciplines).[6]

S. Radhakrishnan who had a great respect for *yoga* wrote:

> It is good to know that the ancient thinkers required of us to realize the possibilities of the soul in solitude and silence, and to transform the flashing and fading moments of vision into a steady light which could illumine the long years of life.

Pranav Pandya says:

> *Yoga* is the process of self-discovery or discovering oneself and developing the divinity latent within oneself.[7]

Swami Ramdev observes:

> *Yoga* is the gradual awakening of the self and the manifestation of divinity within.[8]

Thus after a careful observation of the meaning and definitions of *yoga* we can say that *yoga* is the union of the individual soul with the supreme soul. Just as camphor melts and becomes one with the fire; just as a drop of water when it is thrown into the ocean becomes one with the ocean, the individual soul, when it is purified, when it is freed from lust, greed, hatred and ego, when it becomes sattvic, becomes one with the supreme soul. We can

---

[5] Osborne, 2006, *Ramana Maharshi and the Path of Self-Knowledge*, p. 90.

[6] Shriram Sharma, 1998c, *Vangamaya: Sadhana se Siddhi 2*, p. 2.4.

[7] *Sanskriti Sanchar*, March 2010, pp. 3-4.

[8] Ibid., p. 4.

say that *yoga* is a practical path to self-realization, a means of attaining enlightenment by purifying the entire being, so that the mind–body can experience the absolute reality underlying the illusions of everyday life. *Yoga* can be said to constitute the very essence of the spirituality of India. *Yoga*, the art of right living, has come down to us from our *rishis* from time immemorial. Many different interpretations of the word *yoga* have been handed down over the centuries. One of the classical definitions of *yoga* is "to be one with divine". It does not matter what name we use for the divine – God, Allah, Ishvara, or whatever – anything that brings us closer to understanding that there is a power higher and greater than ourselves is *yoga*. When we feel in harmony with that higher power that too is *yoga*. Thus *yoga* is the science that teaches us the method of uniting the individual soul with the universal soul, of merging the individual will in the cosmic will; of experiencing our oneness with the divine consciousness.

Aim of Yoga

The ultimate aim of *yoga* is to unite the human soul with the universal soul. The aim of *yoga* is to tear the veil that keeps man confined within the human dimension of consciousness. *Yoga* is radically different from the normal consciousness of human beings. This is a point of paramount importance for every seeker of *yoga* to bear in mind – one passes beyond death only on realizing Him. There is no other way to escape from the cycle of births and deaths.[9]

Moreover *yoga* is the only way to sustain one's spiritual reality in the midst of life's turmoil and to discipline one's inner awareness until he attains liberation. *Yoga* can be considered among those highly developed spiritual disciplines that enable man to cope with the tragic developments in life.[10] Normally a man is lost in his own confused thoughts and feelings, but when *yoga* is attained the personal consciousness becomes stilled like a lamp in a windless

---

[9] *Shvetashvatara Upanishad* 3.8.

[10] www.hinduwisdom.in of/yoga and hindu philosophy.htm (17 July 2008).

place and it is then possible for the embodied spirit to know itself as apart from the manifestations to which it is accustomed, and to become aware of its own nature. *Yoga* is, of course, excellent for physical, mental and spiritual well-being. The goal of *yoga* is essentially to cause the mind to become like zero. In fact, the goal of *yoga* is to zero out thoughts, and the mind, and to realize the supreme and become like the supreme.

Shiva Samhita states:

> He who contemplates on *shunya* . . . is absorbed into space . . . think on the great void unceasingly. The great void, whose beginning is void, whose middle is void, (and) whose end is void . . . , by contemplating continually on this, one obtains success, enlightenment.[11]

Yoga Upanishad states:

> Living souls are prisoners of the joys and woes of existence and to liberate them from nature's magic the knowledge of the *Brahman* is necessary. It is hard to acquire, this knowledge, but it is the only boat, to carry one over the river of *samsara*. A thousand are the paths that lead there, yet it is one, in truth, knowledge, the supreme refuge.[12]

Maharshi Aurobindo states:

> As our senses give us the knowledge of the external things by directing our consciousness outwardly, in the same way if we can direct our consciousness inwardly and rise into the inner consciousness, we can know the things of the higher worlds. We have to take an entire turn in our consciousness and go beyond the limitations of our physical senses, then only can we have the true knowledge of this world and the worlds beyond and that practice is called *yoga*.[13]

---

[11] www.hinduwisdom.in of/yoga and hindu philosophy.htm (17 July 2008).

[12] Ibid.

[13] Aurobindo, 2000, *A Practical Guide to Integral Yoga*, p. 4.

He further says:

> By the practice of *yoga*, our consciousness expands as wide as the universe and far beyond. All the systems of *yoga* practised up to now had almost the same goal and purpose. That is to raise the consciousness to a stage of bliss and fix it there.[14]

Mundaka Upanishad 2.39 states:

> He who knows that supreme *Brahman* becomes *Brahman* itself. He swims across grief, crosses over sin.

Yajurveda 13.81 states:

> From the earth I rise to the skies: from the skies I rise to the heavens. From the heavens free of sorrows I reach the light that is freedom. I know the great person shining as the sun beyond darkness. Only upon knowing it supersedes. There is no other path for one to follow.

Kathopanishad 2.3.18 ends with the statement:

> Nachiketa obtained the science and entire method of *yoga* as taught by the God of Death. Attaining *Brahman* be became free of all dust and rose above death; so also anyone who knows this science of the inner self.

Hatha-Yoga Pradipika 1.64-66 states:

> The young, the old, the extremely aged, even the sick obtain perfection in *yoga* by constant practice. Success in *yoga* is not obtained by the mere theoretical reading of sacred texts. Success is not obtained by wearing the dress of a *yogi* or a *sannyasi* (a recluse), nor by talking about. Constant practice alone is the secret of success. Verily, there is no doubt about this.

The aim of *yoga* would become all the more clear to us if we see it in the light of what Maharshi Aurobindo says about it in his *The Yoga and Its Objects* (p. 1):

---

[14] Aurobindo, 2000, *A Practical Guide to Integral Yoga*, p. 4.

> The *yoga* we practise is not for ourselves alone, but for the Divine; its aim is to work out the will of the Divine in the world, to effect a spiritual transformation and to bring down a divine nature and a divine life for the whole humanity. Its object is not personal *mukti*, although *mukti* is a necessary condition of the *yoga*, but the liberation and transformation of the human being.

Thus we find reference to *yoga sadhana* in almost every holy book. Almost every scriptures of India have declared that self-realization is the supreme aim of human life and this can be attained only by the constant practice of *yoga-sadhana*. Ancient Indian literature is full of the elaborate description of such a highest state of being as well as a number of techniques adopted to achieve this final goal. Many great *yogi*s like Sri Ramakrishna Paramahansa, Swami Vivekananda, Swami Ramteertha, Maharshi Aurobindo, Ramana Maharshi and Yugrishi Shriram Sharma Acharya of recent past are some of the glorifying examples of spiritual transformation. The different practices of *yoga sadhana* whether they be *karma-yoga*, *bhakti-yoga*, *jnana-yoga* or *raja-yoga*, they pave the way for the lifting up of human consciousness to a higher and noble realm of light, love and life with divine harmony and joy.

2

History and Traditions of Yoga

TALKING of global Indian heritage, *yoga* is perhaps the most recognized one, having travelled all over the world for every one's well-being. *Yoga* is a legacy of an ancient and continuous 5,000-years old Indian civilization and yet quite modern with the backing of science.

It is said that *yoga* was a divine gift revealed to the ancient sages so that mankind could have the opportunities to realize its divine nature and that the divine tradition of *yoga* began with the very resonance of Vedic *richas* (Vedic *mantras*) in the caves of Devatma Himalayas, and with the very first ray of civilization the divine light of *yoga* spread in human life.[1]

It was slowly evolved and developed by the ancient sages, not only in India but all over the world; because our sages knew that alike the rising sun which illuminates the snow-covered Himalayas, the light of *yoga* would diminish the impudence and ignorance of human life. The reason – the ultimate source of light and power is the Supreme Lord only and the radiance of *yoga* would enlighten not only an individual but the entire mankind.[2]

Generally the teachings of *yoga* were passed on from *gurus* to their disciples. In this way there was a clear understanding of the techniques and aims of *yoga*. For, the *guru*, through his personal experience, could guide his disciples along the right path and keep them away from any confusion on misunderstanding. Through personal experience, realized *yogis* and sages were able to guide

---

[1] *Akhand Jyoti*, September 2001, p. 5.

[2] Ibid.

sincere aspirants along the right path, removing any confusion, misunderstanding and excessive intellectual contemplation. Thus the *yoga* that we know today was being practised in India since time immemorial.[3]

There have been much debate among scholars over the questions like when did *yoga* originate? Who did originate *yoga*?

The Vedas are considered the oldest book of the world. And we have *yogas* in the Vedas. We, of course, find the evidence of *yogis* and *yoga* tradition in hymn — X.136 of *Rigveda* where it describes a long-haired ascetic and his yogic powers. But if we consider the beginning of *yoga* from the Vedas it would not be true. Why? Because the verses of the Vedas were heard by the *rishis*, seers in states of meditation and *samadhi*, and therefore are regarded as revealed scriptures. This shows that even before the Vedas *yoga* existed in the universe in some form or the other.

In *Yajnavalkya Smriti* 125 and *Mahabharata* 12.349.65, Hiranyagarbha is stated as the originator of *yoga*:

> *hiranyagarbho yogasya vakta nanyah puratanah* ।
>
> Hiranyagarbha was the first being to reveal or (to speak of) *yoga*.

In another context in *Mahabharata* 12.342.96, Hiranyagarbha has been described as omnipresent and powerful.

The 121st verse of the 10th *mandala* of *Rigveda* is known as Hiranyagarbha verse. *Ramayana* declares him as the soul of the entire universe.[4] This whole description makes it clear that Vedic tradition accepts *yoga* as the one propounded by God himself. This shows that *yoga* is as old as the universe and has been gifted for the betterment of mankind by God himself. It is said that even Lord Brahma had to perform *tapa* (austerity) to create this universe. And it is a well-known fact that austerity (penance) performed by Lord

---

[3] Saraswati, 2002, *Asana, Pranayama, Mudra, Bandha*, p. 3.

[4] *Adbhut Ramayana* 5.6.

Brahma is nothing but an integral part of *yoga* itself. Highlighting the divine tradition of *yoga,* Goswami Tulsidas writes:

> *tapabala rachayi prapanchu bidhataA tapabala bishnu sakal jaga trata* ||
>
> *tapabala sambhu karahin sangharaA tapabala seshu dharai mahibhara* ||[5]
>
> By the power of penance the creator makes the world; by the power of penance Vishnu protects it, by the power of penance, Shambhu brings about its dissolution; by the power of penance, again, Shesha supports the burden of the earth.

He further writes:

> *tapa adhar sab sristi bhavani* |[6]
>
> In fact, the entire creation, Bhavani rests on penance.

He again highlights the divine tradition of *yoga* when he writes:

> *matu pitahi bahubidhi samujhayi* | *chalin uma tap hit harshayi* |[7]
>
> Then, after consoling her parents in every possible way, Uma gladly went away to practise penance.

How the tradition of *yoga* has been flowing since time immemorial can be understood well in the light of what Lord Krishna says:

> I taught this immortal *yoga* to Vivasvan (sun-God), Vivasvan conveyed it to Manu (his son); and Manu imparted it to (his son) Ikshvaku.[8]
>
> Thus transmitted in succession from father to son.[9]
>
> The same ancient *yoga* has this day been imparted to you

---

[5] *Ramcharitmanas*, Balkanda, 72.2.

[6] Ibid., 72.3.

[7] Ibid., 72.4.

[8] *Gita* IV.1.

[9] Ibid., IV.2.

> (Arjuna) by me, because you are my devotee and friend; and also because this is a supreme secret.[10]

There are said to be three main traditions of *yoga*:

1. *Raja-yoga:* Brahma is considered the creator of the universe. He is also called Adipurusha and Rajapurusha. The *yoga* originated from him is called *raja-yoga*. Maharshi Patanjali, the incarnation of Lord Brahma organized the tradition of *raja-yoga* in a systematic manner in his *Yogasutra*.
2. *Vedic Yoga:* Vishnu (who protects the universe) is considered the originating symbol (or token of) all the Vedas. The *yoga* originated from him is known as Vedic *yoga*. Lord Krishna, the incarnation of Vishnu, is considered the propounder of Vedic *yoga*. It is he who organized the tradition of Vedic *yoga* in a systematic manner. *Srimad Bhagavadgita* is the book establishing and continuing Vedic *yoga*; by Lord Krishna.
3. *Hatha-yoga:* Shiva (who brings about its (universe) dissolution) is considered the propounder of the third tradition of *yoga*. In yogic literatures He is known as the Adinath. The *yoga* which originates from him is called *hatha-yoga*. Gorakhnath is considered the incarnation of Lord Shiva, who for the establishment and orientation of *hatha-yoga* wrote many books on *hatha-yoga*: *Goraksha Shataka*, *Goraksha Paddhati*, *Yoga-bija* and *Siddha Siddhanta Paddhati*.[11]

A careful observation shows that these are the main traditions of *yoga* and all other traditions are merged with these or in other words we can say that these three traditions have incorporated or included in themselves all other traditions of *yoga*.

Thus *yoga* has a long history and its tradition has been transmitted since time immemorial. In archaeological excavations made in the Indus Valley at Harappa and Mohenjo-Daro (the

---

[10] *Gita*, IV.3.

[11] *Yoga Vijnana*, 2008, p. 11.

Harrapan culture can be dated at least as far back as 3300 BCE) now in Pakistan, various statues have been unearthed depicting people practising *yoga*. They show Lord Shiva (the mythological originator of *yoga*) and his consort Parvati sitting in various *asana*s and practising meditation. These ruins were once the dwelling places of people who lived in the pre-Vedic age. These discoveries allow us therefore to speculate with some justification that *yoga* was practised by the people of Indus Valley.[12]

The first books to mention *yoga* were the ancient Vedas. In fact, the verses of the Vedas were revealed by *yogi*s in states of meditation (*samadhi*). It is for this reason that the Vedas are regarded as revealed scriptures. The *rishi*s did not compose the verses but acted as transmitters through which these revelations were expounded. The Vedas are regarded as the first yogic text, for they illustrate, even in an indirect manner, the essence of *yoga*. *Rigveda*, the oldest book in the world, speaks of "yoking the mind to the ultimate truth". The word *yoga* occurs in various forms in the Vedas like *Rigveda* I.34.9, II.8.1, V.43.5. Also the virtues as described in *yama*s and *niyama*s of Patanjali's *ashtanga-yoga* occurs in *Rigveda*. Virtues like *satya*, *ahimsa*, *shaucha*, *tapa*, *svadhyaya* (of *mantra*s) and lastly *ishvara pranidhana* (meditation of God), were the acts of the *rishi*s, who by prayer (*tapa*), surrendered themselves completely to the Almighty power.

The science of sound was clearly recognized by the seers of the Vedas for they mention various *mantra*s that can be used for the attainment of both material as well as spiritual goal. In conclusion, we can say that the concept of *yoga* was known in Vedic times (2000–1500 BCE) in one form or another. During this period the experiences of *yoga* were known but the science of *yoga* was yet to be systematized.[13]

Second, it is with the advent of the Upanishads that we begin

---

[12] www.kamalaya.com

[13] Saraswati, 1989, *Yoga and Kriya*, p. 102.

to see *yoga* assume a more definite shape. The creation of the Upanishads marks the pre-classical *yoga* or Upanishadic (800–100 BCE) *yoga*. The Upanishads explain the subjects like the ultimate reality (*Brahman*), the self (*atman*), and the relationship between the two, and the realization of *Brahman*.

An early reference to meditation is made in *Brihadaranyaka Upanishad*, the earliest Upanishad (approx. 900 BCE). In the last *mantra* of *Ishopanishad* the aspirant for self-realization prays for the removal of veil covering the ultimate truth. This veil is nothing but the ignorance as we have in the *yoga* occurred in Upanishads like *Kena*, *Chhandogya*, *Brihadaranyaka*, *Maitrayani*, *Kaushitaki* and *Shvetashvatara* is no different from *yoga-vidya*.

In *Maitrayani Upanishad* (200–300 BCE) *yoga* surfaces as:

> *Shadanga-yoga* as: Breath control (*pranayama*), sensory inhibition (*pratyahara*), meditation (*dhyana*), concentration (*dharana*), examination (*tarka*) and ecstasy (*samadhi*).[14]

In *Katha Upanishad yoga* surfaces as:

> When the five instruments of knowledge stand still, together with the mind and when intellect does not move, that is called the supreme state. — III.10
>
> This, the firm control of the senses, is what is called *yoga*. — III.11
>
> Having received this wisdom taught by the king of death and the entire process of *yoga*, Nachiketa became free from impurities and death and attained *Brahman*. Thus it will be also with any other who knows, in this manner, the self. — III.18

The essential message of the Upanishads is that the self can only be known through union (*yoga*). Furthermore, it is emphasized again and again that the self is not to be realized outside; it is not something separate, but at the very core of our being. The early

---

[14] www.orientlia.Org/term 3923.html

Upanishads, like the *Kena* and *Isha,* began to indirectly develop and formulate the precepts of *karma-yoga* though it is left to the later *Bhagavadgita* to fully expound the essence of *karma-yoga.* It is these Upanishads that first indicate the possibility of treading the yogic path and reaching the culmination while performing one's everyday duties. Until this time there was a tendency to see the yogic and spiritual paths as being completely separate and divorced from worldly pursuits.[15]

Third, it is *Bhagavadgita* which is a classical book on *yoga. Gita* consists of 700 verses in which Arjuna, a great warrior, is instructed in the practice of *yoga* by Yogeshvara Sri Krishna, incarnation of God, who assumes the role of charioteer during the battle of Kurukshetra. *Bhagavadgita* is a yogic scripture, and is applicable to people throughout the world and in every walk of life. In *Gita* we have the confluence of the yogic paths like *karma-yoga, jnana-yoga* and *bhakti-yoga.* In fact, with regard to *karma-yoga* it can be considered the supreme treatise. It is in *Bhagavadgita* where we really see that *yoga* is for everyone and not for the recluse. Before the writing of this text there was a tendency to regard *yoga* as unworldly and unconnected with daily life. It is *Bhagavadgita* that urges everyone to start practising *yoga* here and now, and not to consider it something to be practised on retirement from one's responsibilities or some time in the future when the opportunity presents itself. It is to be practised now as an integral part of one's life.[16] It is in *Bhagavadgita* II.48 where we have some excellent definitions of *yoga*:

> *samatvam yoga uchyate*
>
> The equality or equanimity is called *yoga.*

Here in the word *samatvam* stands for evenness of mind. It is in this state of mind that one enjoys union.

---

[15] Saraswati, 1989, op. cit., p. 104.

[16] Ibid., p. 105.

One of the best examples that we have in the *Gita* II.50 is:

yogah karmasu kaushalam (*yoga* is skill in action).

Gita accepts actions as the main cause of bondage and rebirth. Hence it is our skill in actions which makes us free from this bondage. The method of salvation taught in *Bhagavadgita* is that a man should live a life of actions without hankering after their results, which should be dedicated to God.

Bhagavadgita occurs in the Bhishma-Parva of *Mahabharata* and comprises eighteen chapters from the 25th to 42nd. Its authorship is traditionally ascribed to Vyasa.[17]

Thus we see the direction and tradition of *yoga* by reference to the ancient texts like Vedas, Upanishads and *Gita*. Here, the most remarkable thing is that before it was systematized, *yoga* was a collection of varied and unrelated techniques, riddled with all types of personal beliefs and superstitions. It is here that the writers of the ancient texts served their greatest purpose by bringing all these different ideas together and integrated them. One of the most successful of these writers was Maharshi Patanjali who wrote the text called *Yogasutra*, 200 BCE. This is still regarded as the classical and authoritative book on *raja-yoga*. In a mere 196 verses, he deals with the essential background, techniques and attainments of *raja-yoga*. In a sense, it can be said that he is the compiler (codifier) more than the writer, for he took all the important existing practices which were used for many centuries up until his time and united them into one comprehensive and harmonious system. He certainly did not invent the path of *raja-yoga* for its constituents were known in essence since the beginning of the Vedic period thousands of years before.[18] Thus without any doubt it can be said that *yoga* has been defined and explained by many *yogis*, saints, scholars and philosophers but it is Maharshi Patanjali to whom goes the credit for systematizing it. When deities and demons churned the ocean,

---

[17] en.wikipedia.org.

[18] Saraswati, 1989, op. cit., p. 105.

they used the mountain Sumeru as the churning rod in the process. From that churning, nectar came out and Lord Vishnu kept it in a jar. Likewise the nectar or *brahma-vidya* was kept by Maharshi Patanjali in a jar which we know as *Yogasutra* of Patanjali.

Thus after *Bhagavadgita*, the next seminal work on *yoga* is *Yogasutra* which was codified sometime between the second century and the third century BCE by Patanjali. Patanjali's *yoga* is known as the *raja-yoga*, which is a system for the control of mind. Patanjali defines *yoga* in his *sutra* 1.2: *yogas chitta-vritti-nirodhah* (*yoga* is restraining the mind stuff from taking various forms). Patanjali's *yoga* is also known as *ashtanga-yoga* (eight-limbed *yoga*). This eight-limbed concept derived from *sutras* 2.29-31 became a feature of *raja-yoga*.

The eight limbs of *yoga* are:

> *Yama* (non-violence, truthfulness, non-stealing, celibacy and non-covetousness or non-possessiveness are five self-restraints), *niyama* (purity, contentment, austerity, self-study and resignation to God are five observances), *asanas* (postures), *pranayama* (breath control), *pratyahara* (withdrawal of the senses from the sense objects), *dharana* (concentration), *dhyana* (meditation) and *samadhi* (liberation).

We see that the whole subject of *raja-yoga* is treated in a most scientific manner starting from moral precepts, leading on to the physical and mental aspects and finally self-realization.

The essential foundations of *yoga* was thus laid down by the time Patanjali had finished writing his *sutras*. Many more texts and developments were to follow, but the structure of *yoga* was outlined; all that was required was the filling in of the empty spaces. This was done mainly by a large number of commentators who interpreted and reinterpreted the traditional texts. Often this caused more confusion than clarity, because many differing commentaries arose resulting in controversy and speculation. Nevertheless a few of these scholars did throw some light on the traditional yogic texts. An example is Shankaracharya, who personally interpreted twelve different Upanishads, and *Bhagavadgita*, as well as wrote many original books on *yoga* such as *Vivekachudamani* (*Crest Jewel of Wisdom*), *Aparokshanubhuti* (*Direct Experience of Reality*) and *Atmabodha* (*Knowledge of the Self*). Shankaracharya was a man who had extensively practised *yoga* for himself and knew by personal experience its significance. He was not therefore to merely analyse intellectually the secret of *yoga* without personal experience. There are many other contributors to the development of *yoga*. Such as *bhakti-yoga*, though practised throughout the eras of *yoga*, was given a particularly strong boost in the middle ages by *bhakti yogi*s like Kabir, Tulsidas and Chaitanya Mahaprabhu. They all wrote wonderful poetry which even now inflames the heart with its devotional feeling. People such as Kabir not only expressed their intense love in their poetry but also interspersed it with clear practical advice on the path of *bhakti-yoga* and other paths.[19]

In the medieval period *hatha-yoga* was evolved and became very popular through the Nath cult. *Hatha-yoga* laid a great emphasis on preparing the body as a vehicle for attaining the higher spiritual experiences. It is this *yoga* which has become so popular throughout the world. Some of the traditional and important texts may be mentioned as *Siddha Siddhanta Paddhati*, *Goraksha Shataka*, *Hatha-Yoga Pradipika*, *Gheranda Samhita*, *Shiva Samhita*, etc.[20] The most well known of them are *Hatha-Yoga Pradipika*, *Shiva Samhita* and *Gheranda Samhita*. These texts give details on *asanas*, *pranayama*, cleansing techniques, *mudras* (gestures), *bandhas* (energy locks), *nada* (meditation on inner sound), *chakras*, etc. All the books emphasize that the *hatha-yoga* practices are not specially aimed at making the body healthy. They are a means to higher ideals, which

---

[19] Saraswati, 1989, op. cit., p. 105.

[20] Ibid., p. 106.

first demand a healthy body.[21] It is said that in the sixth century BCE, when Lord Buddha's influence brought the ideals of meditation, ethics and morality to the fore and the preparatory practices of *yoga* were ignored. The Indian thinkers soon realized the limitations of this view. The *yogi* Matsyendranath taught that before taking to the practices of meditation, the body and its elements need purifying. He thus founded the Nath cult and the yogic pose *matsyendrasana* was named after him.[22] His chief disciple, Gorakhnath wrote books like *Siddha Siddhanta Paddhati* and *Goraksha Shataka* on *hatha-yoga.* One of the most outstanding authorities on *hatha-yoga*, Swami Swatmarama, the disciple of Gorakhnath wrote *Hatha-Yoga Pradipika* in the fifteenth century. In this treatise Swatmarama wrote his own yogic experiences and introduced *hatha-yoga* as a "stairway to the heights of *raja-yoga*, hence a preparatory stage of physical purification that renders the body fit for the practice of higher meditation".[23]

Another classical book written on *hatha-yoga* is *Gheranda Samhita* written by Gheranda Rishi in the seventeenth century. *Gheranda Samhita* is a manual of *yoga* taught by Gheranda to Chandakapali. *Gheranda Samhita* speaks of sevenfold *yoga*: *shatkarma* (for purification), *asana* (for strengthening), *mudra* (for stealing), *pratyahara* (for calming), *pranayama* (for lightness), *dhyana* (for perception) and *samadhi* (for isolation).[24]

Shiva Samhita (or the collection of the knowledge of Shiva) is another manual on *hatha-yoga* (written in the seventeenth century). The first chapter states that it is the *yogi*'s task to realize the unity of the individual self, in order to perceive the true nature of reality. This can only be done by dissolving the veil of *maya*. The second chapter describes certain aspects of the human subtle bodily matrix.

---

[21] Saraswati, 1989, op. cit., p. 106.

[22] Saraswati, 2002, op. cit., p. 4.

[23] www.yogapoint.com

[24] en.wikipedia.org

Third chapter includes some discussion of *pranayama* and *asana*. The fourth chapter is concerned with *mudra*, and the fifth deals with the six major *chakra*s and four aspects of *yoga*, namely, *mantra*, *hatha*, *laya* and *raja-yoga*.[25]

Thus we find that there are many ancient saints, sages and *yogi*s who have contributed to the growth of *yoga*. But unless we refer to the development of *yoga* in modern times, the survey of historical development of *yoga* would not be complete. The age-old tradition of *yoga* continuous even today without any break or uninterrupted. In modern times *yogi*s like Sri Ramakrishna Paramahansa, Swami Vivekananda, Swami Ramteertha, Maharshi Aurobindo, Ramana Maharshi, Swami Satyananda Saraswati, Swami Shivananda, Yugrishi Shriram Sharma Acharya, Swami Rama, Swami Niranjanananda Saraswati and Swami Ramdev made a remarkable contribution in popularizing *yoga*. Let us have a glance at some remarkable *yogi*s of the modern era.

One of the greatest *yogi*s who appeared in the modern era was Sri Ramakrishna Paramahansa (1836-86). He was an embodiment of integral *yoga*. He used to say:

> *Bhakti-yoga*, *jnana-yoga*, *karma-yoga* are the paths by which you can realize God. Whatever path you may follow, you will realize Him, but the path of *bhakti* is an easy one.[26]
>
> There are different ways, in accordance with the nature of aspirants. A man should be given food according to his power of digestion. Suppose a mother has bought a fish for the family, all her children have not the same power of digestion. For some she makes pilau and for others she makes stew. These latter have weak stomachs.

By performing various yogic experiments through different paths he proved that God is one with a thousand names. A lake and as

---

25 www.indianetzone.com

26 Gupta, 2007, *The Gospel of Sri Ramakrishna*, p. 482.

many *ghats*. Not only did he leave behind a luminous trail for those who want to tread the path of self-realization but also for the larger humanity showed the path of serving God man.[27] Later on the spiritual teachings of Sri Ramakrishna Paramahansa was spread globally by his disciples like Swami Vivekananda.

The teachings of Sri Ramakrishna Paramahansa have been very beautifully recorded by Mahendranath Gupta (a disciple of Sri Ramakrishna Paramahansa) in the form of *The Gospel of Sri Ramakrishna*. It is in fact the ocean of *yoga* for spiritual seekers.

Swami Vivekananda (1863–1902) made *yoga* popular worldwide. The ground for its introduction to the West was laid in 1893 when Swami Vivekananda, a great *yogi* and disciple of Sri Ramakrishna Paramahansa, addressed the World Parliament of Religions in Chicago. His books (compiled from lectures given around the world) on the four *yogas*: *raja-yoga*, *karma-yoga*, *bhakti-yoga* and *jnana-yoga* are very influential and still seen as fundamental texts for anyone interested in the practice of *yoga*.[28] He is considered a key figure in the introduction of Indian philosophy and *yoga* in India and abroad. He firmly believed that *yoga* should be promoted in a big way in India reaching out to the masses and not just restricted to the elite. Swamiji was a great advocate of the adoption of *yoga* worldwide.[29]

Another great *yogi* who made a remarkable contribution to the tradition of *yoga* was Maharshi Aurobindo (1872–1950). Sri Aurobindo propagated the practice of integral *yoga*. This is Aurobindo's synthesis of the four main *yogas*: *karma-yoga*, *jnana-yoga*, *bhakti-yoga* and *raja-yoga*. Maharshi Aurobindo taught that the transformation of world-consciousness is possible through a spiritual journey of discipline and *yoga*. He showed us his way of self-discipline through integral *yoga*. His translations and interpretations of yogic scriptures like Upanishads and *Bhagavadgita*

---

27 Gupta, 2007, *The Gospel of Sri Ramakrishna*, p. 855.

28 enwikipedia.org/wiki/swamivivekananda

29 www.narendramodi.in

are considered a remarkable contribution. His writings, notably, *The Synthesis of Yoga; The Essays on the Gita; Savitri; The Secret of the Veda* and *Life Divine* are just the ocean of *yoga* in which any lover of *yoga* can have a yogic bath aimed at self-realization. Even the mother (of the Aurobindo Ashram, popularly known as Sri Ma) contributed a lot by continuing the work of consciousness evolution, leaving a stunning legacy of wisdom, knowledge, realization and impulses for making the integral *yoga* physically effective, in a life where spirit and matter are one. Sri Aurobindo's yogic legacy has survived and is thriving internationally today.[30]

Ramana Maharshi (30 December 1879 – 14 April 1950) remains one of the most important *yogis* of the modern era and his realization (I am that) inspires the masses even today. It was in 1911 that the first Westerner, Frank Humphreys, then a policeman stationed in India, discovered Sri Ramana and wrote articles about him which were first published in the *International Psychic Gazette* in 1913. Sri Ramana became well known in and out of India after 1934 when Paul Brunton, having first visited Sri Ramana in January 1931, published the book *A Search in Secret India*, which became very popular. Sri Ramana's fame spread throughout the 1840s. Sri Ramana's teachings about self-enquiry, the practice he is most widely associated with, have been classified as the path of knowledge (*jnana-yoga*).

The purest form of his teachings was the powerful silence which radiated from his presence and quieted the minds of those who attuned to it. He gave verbal teachings only for the benefit of those who could understand his silence (or, perhaps, could not understand how to attain the silent state). His verbal teachings were said to flow from his direct experience of consciousness (*atman*) as the only existing reality. When asked for advice, he recommended self-enquiry as the fastest path to *moksha*.

Although he advocated self-enquiry as the fasted means to

---

30 http: //www.Boloji.com

realization, he also recommended the path of *bhakti* and self-surrender (to one's deity or *guru*) and gave his approval to a variety of paths and practices.[31] He observed:

> The mind will subside only by means of the enquiry "Who am I?" The thought "Who am I?", destroying all other thoughts, will itself finally be destroyed like the stick used for stirring the funeral pyre.

Over the course of Sri Ramana's lifetime, people from a wide variety of backgrounds, religions and countries were drawn to him. Some stayed for the rest of their lives (or his) and served him with great devotion, and others came for a single *darshan* and left, deeply affected by peace he radiated.

A number of followers wrote books conveying Sri Ramana's teachings. Sri Muruganar (1893–1973) recorded the most comprehensive collection of Sri Ramana's sayings in a work called *Guru Vachaka Kovai* (*Garland of Guru's Sayings*). Sri Muruganar was also instrumental in Sri Ramana's writing of *Upadeshasaram* (*Essence of Instruction*) and *Ulladu Narpadu* (*Forty Verses on Reality*).

Sri Sadhu Om's (1922-85) understanding of Sri Ramana's teachings on self-enquiry is explained in his *The Path of Sri Ramana* (Part 1):

> Suri Nagamma wrote a series of letters to her brother in Telugu, describing Sri Ramana's conversations with devotees over a five- year period. Each letter was corrected by Sri Ramana before it was sent. Paul Brunton's writings like *A Search in Secret India* brought considerable attention to him in the West.[32]

Swami Shivananda (1887–1963) was another great *yoga* master of modern times. He was known to have said:

> An ounce of practice is better than tons of theory. Practise

---

31 http://en.wikipedia.org/wiki/raman-maharshi

32 http://en.wikipedia.org/wiki/raman-maharshi

> *yoga*, religion and philosophy in daily life and attain self-realization.[33]
>
> He called his *yoga* the *yoga* of synthesis. He wrote hundreds of books and articles on *yoga* and spirituality to maintain and introduce yogic values in the minds of the general public. His emphasis was on breaking down the barriers which separated the needy from the teachings that could help them, whether this took the form of *yoga* for health, peace of mind or spiritual aspiration.

This ideology continues to guide the work of the Satyananda branch of his lineage. Swami Shivananda toured India, inspiring people to practise *yoga* and lead a divine life. He founded the Divine Life Society in Rishikesh in 1936. A great spiritual luminary of the twentieth-century Swami Shivananda Saraswati developed *yoga* as a practical, integrated subject which everyone could apply in their lives. Embodying the spirit of service to humanity, he inspired people to practise *yoga* and lead a divine life. His eightfold path – serve, love, give, purify, be good, do good, meditate, realize – became a roadmap for spiritual aspirants worldwide. By founding the International Yoga Fellowship (in 1956) and the Bihar School of Yoga (in 1963) Swami Satyananda Saraswati the close disciple of Swami Shivananda hoisted the flag of *yoga* in every corner of the world and authored over eighty major texts on *yoga* and spiritual life. Swami Niranjanananda Saraswati, a disciple of Swami Satyananda Saraswati, authoring many classic books on *yoga*, Tantra and Upanishads and going on numerous national and international tours for many years, provided practical guidance and inspiration to live a yogic lifestyle, develop spiritual awareness for aspirants the world over.[34]

Another great *yogi* who appeared in this era was Paramahansa Yogananda (1893–1952). He was a practitioner of *kriya-yoga*. Paramahansa Yogananda describes *kriya-yoga* as the "airplane route

---

33 http://en.wikipedia.org/wiki/swami sivananda

34 www.satyananda ashram.gr/en

to God". *Tapa* (penance), *svadhyaya* (self-study), *ishvara pranidhana* (devotion) together form *yoga. Kriya-yoga* is not a matter of doing but of being aware of everything that one may be doing. The teachings of *kriya-yoga* given by Paramahansa Yogananda can be practised by all sincere seekers, both householder devotees and *sannyasis*. Direct perception of God through the practice of *kriya-yoga* is the main plank of the teachings of Paramahansa Yogananda. Known as the "Father of Yoga in the West", the great spiritual *guru* spent thirty-two years in the West. Spreading *yoga* and spirituality is India's immortal gift to the rest of the world.[35]

His Guru Swami Yukteshvarananda Giri (the disciple of Lahiri Mahashaya) who trained Paramahansa Yogananda in *kriya-yoga*, explained:

> The West is high in material attainments, but lacking in spiritual understanding. It is God's will that you (Paramahansa Yogananda) play a role in teaching mankind the value of balancing the material with an inner, spiritual life.[36]

Today the *kriya-yoga* teachings of the great master Paramahansa Yogananda are being spread in India and abroad by Yogada Satsang Society of India, the institution founded by Yogananda in 1917 to propagate his teachings on *kriya-yoga*. Autobiography of a *yogi*, written by Paramahansa Yogananda is the spiritual classic for the spiritual seekers, today. Other books propagating *yoga* are *Yogiraj Shyama Charan Lahiri Mahashaya* and *Purana Purusha: Yogiraj Sri Shyama Charan Lahiri* published by Yogiraj Publication. Among others are the *Holy Science*, written by Yukteshvarananda Giri. A collection of *Biography of 4 Kriya Yoga Gurus*, published by Yogada Satsang Society.[37]

Under the guidance of Paramahansa Yogananda, the personal

---

35 www.articles+base.com>spirituality>religion.

36 http://www. ananda.org/ananda/lineage/kriyananda

37 http://en.wikipedia.org/wiki mahavatar—baba ji

guidance and instruction that he had given to students of his classes in *raja-yoga* during the years 1920 through 1952 were arranged into a comprehensive series of lessons. The Yogada Satsang lessons were meant for study and practice in privacy of one's home.[38]

Another great *yogi* who appeared in this era was Yugrishi Shriram Sharma Acharya (1911-90). In recent history of India Yugrishi made an attempt to revive the tradition of *rishi*s (*rishi-parampara*). He accomplished the Herculean task of reviving the tradition of *rishi*s under the guidance of his Guru Sri Sarveshvarananda Ji, the great Himalayan *yogi*. History bears testimony to the fact that Yugrishi spent his lifetime in rigorous penance and succeeded in reviving the traditions of great *rishi*s like Vishvamitra, Vyasa, Patanjali, Parashurama, Bhagiratha, Charaka, Yajnavalkya, Narada and Shankaracharya. In fact, his yogic personality touched the Himalayan peaks. "Arousal of divinity within man and heaven on earth" – this was the ultimate goal of his life. He founded All World Gayatri Pariwar (that means the whole world is my family – *vasudhaiva kutumbakam*), Shantikunj, founded by him at Haridwar in 1971 is working for the spiritual renaissance of the globe.

His emphasis was on breaking down the barriers of caste, creed, colour as all the beings are the children of the same God. A great spiritual luminary of the twentieth century, Yugrishi Shriram Sharma Acharya developed *yoga* as a practical subject which everyone could apply in their lives. Embodying the spirit of service to humanity, he inspired people to practise *yoga* and lead a divine life. His threefold path of Upasana–Sadhana–Aradhana (USA) became a roadmap for spiritual aspirants worldwide. He authored over 3,000 books in his lifetime. Yugrishi's translations and interpretations of yogic scriptures like Vedas, Upanishads, Puranas, *Ramayana*, *Bhagavadgita*, Yoga Darshan and the books written by him like *Main Kya Hun*, *Gayatri Mahavijnana*, *Sadhana*

---

[38] www.articles+base.com>spirituality>religion

Paddhatiyon ka Jnana-Vijnana, Sukshmikarana Sadhana, Meri Vasiyat aur Virasat, Sunsan ke Sahchara are the classic texts on *yoga* for spiritual seekers.[39]

Pranav Pandya drawn to spiritual life from an early age surrendered himself to Yugrishi Shriram Sharma Acharya in Shantikunj, Haridwar who initiated him. The spiritual teachings of the great master Yugrishi are being spread globally by him. Through authoring many classic books on *yoga* and spirituality like *Antar Jagat ki Yatra ka Jnana-Vijnana, Yug Gita, Chetna ki Shikhar Yatra, The Pioneers of Scientific Spirituality* and *Sishya Sanjivini*, and going on numerous national and international tours for years, he has provided practical guidance and inspiration to live a yogic lifestyle and to develop spiritual awareness for aspirants, the world over.

Swami Ramdev is a modern *yogi* who has contributed a lot in spreading *yoga* worldwide. While the important aspects of *pranayama* was neglected due to its lack of popularity and fear of potential negative side effects, Swami Ramdev has broadcast teachings about it through TV channels and held mass campaigning's in India and world over.[40] He is travelling globally to spread the message of *yoga*. Swami Ramdev has really emerged as a notable personality in the world sphere for his contributions in *yoga*. It was a historic day when the Prime Minister of India, Mr Narendra Modi during his speech at the United Nations General Assembly (UNGA), on 27 September 2014 said:

> *Yoga* is an invaluable gift of India's ancient tradition. It embodies unity of mind and body; thought and action; restraint and fulfilment; harmony between man and nature; a holistic approach to health and well-being. It is not about exercise but to discover the sense of oneness with yourself, the world and the nature. By changing our lifestyle and creating consciousness, it can help in well-

---

[39] www.awgp.org

[40] www.spiritus_temporis.com/great_morden_yogis

> being. Let us work towards adopting an International Yoga Day.

Following this proposal the International Day of Yoga (IYD) was declared unanimously by UNGA. 21 June was declared as IYD. Since its inception in 2015, 21 June is celebrated as IYD. And it is creating a new record of popularity of *yoga* every year.[41]

The age-old traditions of *yoga* are like the ever-flowing holy Ganges. The list of the *yogi*s is endless. The number of *yoga* books runs into thousands. We have only given a quick glimpse of the history and traditions of *yoga*. To sum up, *yoga* (which is a way of living, a divine pathway to a healthy and pure body, mind and soul) has become an integral part of Indian culture and tradition.

---

[41] wikipedia.org/wiki/IYD

3

Different Paths of Yoga

THERE are different paths of *yoga*, all leading to the same goal of self-realization. All the paths of *yoga* are like different spokes of a wheel, they all meet at the same centre: self-realization. Let us briefly discuss of these different paths.

Raja-Yoga

Raja-yoga refers to the system of *yoga* that is described in *Yogasutra* of Patanjali. In this ancient text Patanjali describes eight stages of *yoga* which are known collectively as *raja-yoga*.[1]

Patanjali in his *Yogasutra* 2.29 says:

> *yamaniyamasanapranayamapratyaharadharanadhyana-samadhayoashtavangani.*
>
> *Yama*, *niyama*, *asana*, *pranayama*, *pratyahara*, *dharana*, *dhyana* and *samadhi* are the steps of *ashtanga-yoga*.

Swami Vivekananda says:

> The science of *raja-yoga* proposes to lay down before humanity a practical and scientifically worked out method for reaching the truth.[2]

A *raja-yogi* ascends the yogic ladder through the eight steps and gets ethical training in the beginning to purify himself by the practice of *yama* and *niyama*. Then he steadies his posture and practises *pranayama* to steady his mind and purify the *nadis*. Thereafter by the practice of *pratyahara*, *dharana* and *dhyana* he

---

[1] www.yoga-ez-fitness-wear.com/yoga-styles

[2] www.hinduwisdom.info/yoga and hinduphilosophy.htm (17 July 2008).

gets *samadhi.*[3]

Thus *raja-yoga* provides an integral eightfold approach or eight limbs (*ashtanga*) for the development of consciousness, finally paving the way for self-realization. The eight limbs of *yoga* are: *yama* (social code of conduct), *niyama* (personal code of conduct), *asana* (physical posture), *pranayama* (control over breathing), *pratyahara* (control of the senses), *dharana* (concentration), *dhyana* (meditation) and *samadhi* (absorption).[4]

We can say that *raja-yoga* is the science of concentrating the mind. The powers of the mind are like rays of dissipated light; when concentrated, they illumine. This is the only means of knowledge.[5] A mind which lacks concentration can never be a fit instrument for the realization of truth. At moments when a man's mind is perfectly calm and still, the truth sometime suddenly dawns on him even though he has not consciously sought for it. When there is no movement of the waters in a lake, when no waves or ripples disturb the surface, the moon is clearly reflected. In the same way, when the mind is not agitated by wandering thoughts, it is possible for it to glimpse the truth. Therefore *raja-yoga* starts with mind. Its goal is complete stilling of the mind, so that the light of the indwelling spirit may shine out, leading to the royal path of self-realization.[6]

Hatha-Yoga

The word *hatha* is made up of two *bija mantras*: *ha* and *tha*. *Ha* stands for the sun or *pingala nadi* and *tha* for the moon or *ida nadi*. Basically the union of these two *nadis* is called *hatha-yoga*. When *ida* and *pingala* unites together the *prana* starts flowing into *sushumna* and the dormant power *kundalini*, which is lying in the *muladhara chakra* awakens, rises and enters *sushumna* and passing through all the six *chakras* reaches the highest peak *brahmarandhra* or *sahasrara*, and

---

[3] Shivananda, 1999a, *Raja Yoga*, p. 12.

[4] Frawley, 2004, *Yoga and Ayurveda*, p. 50.

[5] www.hinduwisdom.info/yoga and hinduphilosophy

[6] Pavitrananda, 2000, *Common Sense about Yoga*, p. 57.

attain the oneness. This is the union of Shakti and Shiva or *Atman* and *Parmatman*. This process destroys the ignorance of the aspirant and illuminates his heart and soul.

The *hatha-yoga* includes a number of physical exercises that aim at rendering the body fit for meditation. By these exercises, the body is tuned so that it absorbs a greater quantity of cosmic energy. This technique disciplines the body and helps in rousing the untapped spiritual energy and uniting the individual soul with the universal soul.[7]

Hatha-yoga also called *hatha-vidya,* is a system of *yoga* introduced by Yogi Swatmarama, a sage of fifteenth-century India, and the compiler of the *Hatha-Yoga Pradipika.*[8] Traditionally, Lord Shiva is credited with propounding *hatha-yoga*. It is said that on a lonely island, assuming nobody else would hear Him, He gave the knowledge of *hatha-yoga* to Goddess Parvati, but a fish heard the entire discourse, remaining still throughout. Lord Shiva took mercy on the fish (*matsya*) and made him a *siddha*, who came to be known as Matsyendranath. Matsyendranath taught *hatha-yoga* to Chaurangi, a limbless man who was given hands and feet by Matsyendranath just by looking at him. *Hatha-yoga* includes *asana, pranayama, mudra, bandha* and *nadanusandhan*. *Hatha-yoga Pradipika* mentions Adinath, Matsyendranath, Gorakhnath and many other *yogi*s who became famous *hatha-yogis*.[9]

Mantra-Yoga

Mantra-yoga is the union of the individual soul with the supreme soul by the chanting of *manta.*[10] *Mananat trayate iti mantrah* – by *manana* (constant thinking or recollection) of which one is released from the bondage of birth and death, is *mantra.*[11] It is said that one can

---

[7] Pavitrananda, 2000, op. cit., p. 57.

[8] en.wikipedia.org/wiki/hatha yoga

[9] Ibid.

[10] Hariharananda, 2008, *Kriya Yoga*, p. 53.

[11] www.yoga-age.com/amrita/mantra.html

achieve the ultimate salvation or union with supreme consciousness by chanting the *mantras*, the aim of the *mantra-yoga.*[12]

The *mantra* itself is a *devata* (deity), manifesting in a sound body. Constant repetition of the *mantra* with faith, devotion and purity bestows on the aspirant illumination, peace, eternal bliss and salvation. By constant repetition of the *mantra* the aspirant imbibes the virtues and powers of the deity that presides over the *mantra. Mantras* are in the form of praise and appeal to the deities, craving for help and mercy.

For example the chanting of Gayatri Mantra bestows on the aspirants discrimination and salvation. Recitation of Surya Mantra bestows health, long life, vigour, brilliance. Recitation of *Adityahridaya Stotram* in the early morning is highly beneficial. Lord Rama conquered Ravana through the recitation of this *stotram* imparted by Agastya Rishi. Rhythmical vibrations of sound give rise to forms. Recitation of the *mantras* gives rise to the formation of the particular figure of the deity.[13]

In fact, *mantra-yoga* is an exact science. Every *mantra* has a *rishi* to whom it was revealed for the first time and who gave this *mantra* to the world. He is the *drashta* (seer) for this *mantra.* Sage Vishvamitra is the *rishi* of Gayatri Mantra. Second, the *mantra* has a metre (*chhanda*), which governs the inflection of the voice. Third, the *mantra* has a particular *devata* (a supernatural being), as its informing power. This *devata* is the presiding deity of the *mantra.* Fourth, the *mantra* has a *bija* (seed) which gives a special power to the *mantra.* The *bija* is the essence of the *mantra.* Fifth, every *mantra* has the *shakti.* The *shakti* is the energy of the form of *mantra,* i.e. of the vibration forms set up by its sound. These carry the man to the *devata* that is worshipped. The devotees get *darshan* of the *ishta devata* (deity).[14]

---

12 www.yoga-ez-fitness-wear.com/yoga-styles.html

13 www.yoga-age.com/amrita/manta.html

14 www.disha.org/teachings/japayoga.htm (20 January 2008).

Laya-Yoga

Laya-yoga is the complete absorption of the mind. The mind is absorbed in the divine *om* sound, which is the cosmic sound of vibration within.[15] In the highest ecstatic state, *vasanas*, *samskaras* are neutralized, preparing the mind for its own dissolution or absorption.[16] *Laya-yoga* is the *yoga* of absorption. It underscores absorption in meditation, merging the mind and breath in the divine. In this practice the *yogi* immerses himself in the universe, becoming a part of the universal body.[17] *Laya-yoga* is a form of *yoga* that focuses on listening to *nada* (inner sounds), which can be heard even with closed ears. *Nada* comes in different variations, ranging from bee hums to ocean waves. By focusing on *nada*s, the mind will become relaxed, and will be oblivious to different distractions around. *Laya-yoga* makes it possible to go through difficulties and overcome negativities, thus it is called the *yoga* of absorption. *Laya- yoga* retains the transcendental self after *yogi*s dissolve themselves meditatively.

The spiritual goal of *laya-yoga* is to achieve the blissful state. Through *laya-yoga*, one can be unified with God, connecting with the consciousness of the divine. In *laya-yoga* different positions, which include sitting, standing, lying and walking, are performed and combined with the right prayers, visualization and breathing techniques. *Sthula kriya*s, rituals, movements are also performed. Transcendental running is also performed by *laya-yogi*s. *Laya-yoga*, in essence, is a mystic method. This is considered as the higher stage of *hatha-yoga* and as one of the grand spiritual paths.[18]

Karma-Yoga

Karma-yoga means the union with God through selfless actions. *Karma* is literally translated as "action" which everyone in this

---

[15] Hariharananda, 2008, op. cit., p. 73.

[16] Feurstein, 2002, *The Yoga Tradition*, p. 73.

[17] *Hatha-Yoga Pradipika* 4.34.

[18] www.abc.of-yoga.com

world performs, whether consciously or unconsciously. When the word *yoga* is added to the word *karma*, it means that any action performed without associating oneself with the fruits of the *karma*. Actually it denotes an inner attitude towards action.[19] The action performed without ego or expectation of any return is *karma-yoga*. One loses his identity while working, only selfless work remains. This state is very difficult to achieve. Generally some rewards or outcomes follow the work and one is attached to this reward or incentive. This is not the *karma-yoga*. Non-attachment with the work and becoming the perfect instrument of the superconsciousness in this manifested universe is the ultimate aim of *karma-yoga*.[20]

Swami Pavitrananda says:

> The art of detachment, by which we can govern all our activities so that we may not be entangled in the meshes of work, though we are engaged in it, is called *karma-yoga*.[21]

Swami Niranjanananda Saraswati says:

> Any action that is performed with a meditative awareness becomes *karma-yoga*.[22]

Yugrishi Shriram Sharma Acharya says:

> Whatever is being done is for the God — when such a feeling springs within oneself — be sure that *karma-yoga* has arrived in one's life.[23]

Swami Ramakrishna Paramahansa says:

> If one serves God through all beings without seeking any return, then he truly performs selfless work, and through such selfless work he does good to himself. This is called

---

[19] Saraswati, 1999a, *Yoga Darshan*, p. 54.

[20] www.yoga-ez-fitness-wear.com/yogastyles.html

[21] Pavitrananda, 2000, p. 28.

[22] Saraswati, 1999a, op. cit., p. 54.

[23] *Akhand Jyoti*, September 2001, p. 11.

> *karma-yoga*. This, too, is a way to realize God.[24]

Lord Krishna in *Gita* II.48 says:

> Arjuna, perform your duties established in *yoga*, renouncing attachment, and even tempered in success and failure. Equanimity in success and failure is *yoga*.

Again in verse II.50 he says:

> Endowed with equanimity, one sheds in this life both good and evil. Therefore, strive for the practice of this *yoga* of equanimity. Skill in action lies in *yoga*.

PRACTICE OF KARMA-YOGA

By the practice of *karma-yoga* a person gains divine experience and perceives that though he is acting, God is the sole doer. Thus *karma-yoga* can be practised every moment of the day offering the fruits of the *karma* to God. This is what Lord Krishna says to Arjuna in *Gita* II.47:

> *karmanyevadhikaraste ma phaleshu kadachan* ।
>
> Your right is to work only, but never to the fruit thereof.

In *Gita* IX.28 Lord Krishna says to Arjuna that by offering the fruits of the action to Him he will be freed from the bondage of *karma*:

> *shubhashubhaphalairevam mokshyase karmbandhanaih* ।
>
> With your mind thus established in the *yoga* of renunciation (offering of all actions to me), you will be freed from them, you will attain me.

And by following this path how a *karma-yogi* remains untouched by sin and finally attains God-realization can be seen in *Gita* V.10, 12:

> *brahmanyadhay karmani sangam tyaktva karoti yah* ।
> *lipyate na sa papena padmapatramivambhasa* ॥
> *yuktah karmaphalam tyaktva shantimapnoti naishthikim* ।
> *ayuktah kamakarena phale sakto nibadhyate* ॥

[24] Gupta, 2007, *The Gospel of Sri Ramakrishna*, p. 671.

Which implies that he who acts offering all actions to God, and shaking off attachment, remains untouched by sin as the lotus leaf by water. By offering the fruit of actions to God, the *karma-yogi* attains everlasting peace in the shape of God-realization, whereas, he who works with a selfish motive, being attached to the fruit of actions through desire, gets tied down.

Thus *Gita* teaches that one who has purified the mind by the practice of *karma-yoga* gains direct knowledge of the self, which leads to liberation.

Swami Shivananda says:

> The practice of *karma-yoga* does not demand that you should possess enormous wealth. You can serve with your mind and body. If you find a poor sick man lying on the roadside, give him some water or milk to drink. Cheer him up with sweet, encouraging words. Put him in a carriage and take him to the nearest hospital, if you have no money to pay for the carriage, carry the patient on your back and see that he is admitted into the hospital. If you do service like this, your heart will be purified. God is more pleased with such sort of service for the poor than with the service done by the rich people with pomp and vanity.[25]

The most remarkable thing for the practitioner of *karma-yoga* is what Swami Vivekananda writes in his book *Karma Yoga*:

> The good deeds should be performed and never spoken about. In the same manner all duties should be performed with the sense that they are offerings to God. Man should realize that he is only an instrument of God. This is what *Bhagavadgita* refers to as *nishkama karma* (duty without attachment). Such selfless man may live in the very heart of a crowded and sinful city, but he will be untouched by sin just as lotus leaf remains untouched by water.
>
> If the householder dies in battle fighting for his country

[25] www.dlshq.org/teachings/karmayoga.htm (20 February 2005).

or his religion, he comes to the same goal as the *yogi* by meditation. If we read the Vedas, we will find this word always repeated – "fearless" – fear nothing. Fear is a sign of weakness. A man must go about his duties without taking notice of the sneers and the ridicule of the world. By work alone men may get to where Buddha got largely by meditation or Christ by prayer. Buddha was a working *jnani*; Christ was a *bhakta* (devotee), but the same goal was reached by both of them.[26]

Jnana-Yoga

Jnana-yoga is the *yoga* of wisdom. This path emphasizes on the true knowledge regarding the nature of the self. Since ignorance (obscures) the self from achieving salvation, the aim of this path is to destroy ignorance by discrimination and contemplation on Truth.[27] Lord Krishna in *Gita* 4.38 says:

> *na hi jnanena sadrisham pavitramih vidyate* ।
>
> Nothing indeed purifies in this world like wisdom. He who lives in self-harmony finds it (wisdom) in time within himself, by himself.

Disclosing the true nature of the self Lord Krishna in the second chapter of *Gita* says:

> *ajo nityah shashvato 'yam purano na hanyate hanyamane sharire* ।। — II.20
>
> *vedavinashinam nityam ya enamajamavyayam* ।
> *katham sa purushah partha kam ghatyati hanti kam* ।। — II.21
>
> *nityah sarvagatah sthanurchalo 'yam sanatanah* ।। — II.24
>
> The soul is never born nor dies; nor does it become only after being born. For it is unborn, eternal, everlasting and ancient; even though the body is slain, the soul is not.
>
> The man who knows this soul to be imperishable, eternal

[26] www.dlshq.org/teachings/karmayoga.htm (20 February 2005).

[27] Vivekananda, 2007, *Karma Yoga*.

> and free from birth and decay, how and whom will he cause to be killed, how and whom will he kill?
>
> As this soul is eternal, omnipresent, immovable, constant and everlasting.

Now the question arises before a practitioner of *jnana-yoga*. Who can attain this true knowledge? Lord Krishna very beautifully answers this question in *Gita* 4.39:

> *shradhavam llabhate jnanam tat-parah samyatendriyah* ।
> *jnanam labdhva param shantim achirenadhigachchhati* ।।
>
> He, who has mastered his senses, is exclusively devoted to his practice and is full of faith attains knowledge; having had the revelation of truth, he immediately attains supreme peace (in the form of God-realization).

Acharya Shankara is of the opinion that ignorance is the sole cause of the bondage and self-knowledge is the cause of liberation from that bondage. Hovering between the cycle of life and death is bondage. Shankara believes in three types of *karma*: *prarabdha karma* (actions of the past bearing its fruits at present), *sanchit karma* (actions of the past but still accumulated), *sanchiyaman kriyaman karma* (actions of the present which will bear its fruits in future). It is the bondage of these *karmas* which binds the person and because of which he goes on suffering/facing lots of miseries.[28] Therefore the person needs the self-knowledge to destroy this bondage. This is what Lord Krishna says in *Gita* IV.37:

> *jnanagni sarvakarmani bhasmasatkurute tatha* ।।
>
> As the blazing fire turns the fuel to ashes, even so the fire of knowledge turns all actions to ashes.

Sri Ramakrishna Paramahansa says:

> The *jnana-yoga* is the path by which a man can realize the true nature of his own self; it is the awareness that Brahma

---

[28] Sharma, 1987, *Indian Philosophy*, p. 219.

> alone is his true nature.[29]

The *jnani*, sticking to the path of knowledge, always reasons about the reality, saying "not this", "not this" and reasoning in this way, the mind becomes steady. Then it disappears and the aspirant goes into *samadhi*. This is the knowledge of *Brahman*. He says further:

> A house without light indicates poverty. So one must light the lamp of knowledge in his own heart: O Lord, be gracious and turn the light of knowledge on thyself, so that I may see thy face.[30]

He continues:

> "Reject what is false; and with a keen sense of discrimination seek what is true." The *jnani*, like a valiant fighter, refuses to identify him with anything that is unreal. He analyses everything belonging to the sense-world as "*neti, neti* — not this, not this", and with a sheer effort of the will, keeps himself unattached to anything that is of a transitory nature. Because he finds on analysis that all earthly desires and relationships possess only a temporary value, he guards himself constantly against the danger of succumbing to their influence. Knowing that his physical body will perish sooner or later, he always tries to kindle in himself the consciousness of his separateness from the body. When a person thus rejects everything that is not real, what remains as the residue is the self or reality.[31]

Thus we can say that *jnana-yoga* is the process of self-realization through illuminative wisdom (self-knowledge). It is not a method by which we try to find rational answers to eternal questions; rather it is a part of meditation leading to self-enquiry and self-realization.[32] *Jnana-yoga* teaches that God is everywhere and in everything. It

---

[29] Gupta, 2007, op. cit., p. 671.

[30] Ibid., p. 133.

[31] Ibid., p. 174.

[32] Pavitrananda, 2000, op. cit., p. 45.

does not differentiate between the self and God.

When the *jnana-yogi* realizes the truth, he feels that the universe is full of God; above, below, and in between. He is in all beings and all beings are in Him. He is *Brahman*, the one spirit of the Universe. It is the body that eats and drinks and experiences pleasures and pain. He is not the body; He is it. He is the witness in health and disease. He is existence, knowledge and bliss. He is the essence of all knowledge. He is eternal and unchanging. Thus through the practice of this path the *yogi*, becomes established in universal consciousness.[33]

Bhakti-Yoga

Bhakti-yoga is the path by which God may be realized through love and devotion. The term *bhakti* comes from the root *bhaj*, which means "to be attached to God". *Bhakti* is an intense devotion and supreme attachment to God. It is pure, unselfish, divine love. There is not a bit of bargaining or expectation here. This pure love leads the devotee to an eternal union with God. Let me quote some great *yogis* who have defined *bhakti-yoga* in their own ways,

Swami Vivekananda says:

> *Bhakti-yoga* is a real, genuine search after the Lord, a search beginning, continuing and ending in love. One single moment of the madness of extreme love to God brings us eternal freedom.[34]

Yugrishi Shriram Sharma Acharya used to say:

> *Nishtha* leads to *bhakti*, *bhakti*, when mature, becomes *bhava*, *bhava*, when concentrated becomes *mahabhava*, and last of all is *prema*. *Prema* is like a cord, by *prema* God is bound to the devotee; he can no longer run away.[35]

---

33 Pavitrananda, 2000, *Common Sense about Yoga*, p. 45.

34 Vivekananda, 2001, *Bhakti Yoga*, p. 4.

35 Shriram Sharma, 2010, *Bhakti-Yoga*, p. 3.

He says:

> *Jnana* when mature becomes *bhakti* and the *bhakti-yoga* is the supreme love for God.[36]

Swami Shivananda says:

> *Bhakti* is love for love's sake. The devotee wants God and God alone. Therefore it is called *param prem rupa.*[37]

Swami Satyanand Saraswati says:

> *Bhakti-yoga* is a *yoga* of devotion or complete faith. This faith is in the God or supreme consciousness in any of the forms. It may be Lord Rama, Krishna, Christ, Mohammed, Buddha, etc. It may be a *guru* for his disciples. Important thing is that the person interested in following this path should have very strong emotional bond with the object of faith. The flow of emotional energy is directed to this object. Mostly people suppress their emotions and that often reflects in the form of physical and mental disorders. This *bhakti-yoga* releases those suppressed emotions and brings the purification of the inner self. Gradually the practitioner looses the self-identity and becomes one with the object of faith; this is a state of self-realization.[38]

Lord Krishna speaks of four types of devotees in *Gita* VII.16-17:

> Four types of devotees of noble deeds worship me, Arjuna, the seeker after worldly possessions, the afflicted, the seeker for knowledge and the man of wisdom.
>
> Of these the best is man of wisdom ever established in identity with me, and possessed of exclusive devotion. For I am extremely dear to the wise man (who knows me in reality), and he is extremely dear to me.

Bhakti is of various kinds. One classification is *sakama bhakti* and

---

[36] Shriram Sharma, 2010, op. cit., p. 4.

[37] www.disha.org/teachings/bhaktiyoga

[38] Saraswati, 2001, *Bhakti Yoga Sagar*, vol. 2, pp. 1-2.

nishkama bhakti. *Sakama bhakti* is devotion with desire for material gains. A man wants wealth and with this motive practises *bhakti*. Another man wants freedom from diseases and therefore does *japa* and offers prayers. This is *sakama bhakti*. Through this *bhakti*, one can have material gains but not self-realization. It is *nishkama bhakti* by which the devotee attains self-realization; as this *bhakti* is love for love's sake. The *bhakta* pours out his heart's love to the Lord.

Another classification of *bhakti* is *apara-bhakti* and *para-bhakti*. *Apara-bhakti* is for beginners in *yoga*. The beginner decorates an image with flowers and garlands, offers *naivedya* (food offerings), wave lights; he observes rituals and ceremonies. The devotee here regards the Lord as a supreme person, who is immanent in that image and who can be propitiated through that form only. Till now he has no expanded heart. But gradually from *apara-bhakti*, the devotee goes to *para-bhakti*, the highest form of *bhakti*.

The devotee who is overpowered by this higher form of *bhakti* is too near the God of love. He sees the Lord and the Lord alone everywhere and feels his power manifest as the entire universe:

> Thou art all-pervading; on what throne shall I seat Thee? Thou art the supreme light, in whose borrowed light the sun, the moon, the stars and the fire shine; shall I wave this little *deepa* of light before you? — Thus the devotee recognizes the transcendental nature of God.[39]

This is what Ramakrishna Paramahansa used to say:

> Cry to the Lord with an intensely yearning heart and you will certainly see him. People shed a whole jug of tears for wife and children. They swim in tears for money. But who weeps for God? Cry to Him with a real cry.[40]

Here in I would like to quote what Ramakrishna Paramahansa used to sing:

---

[39] www.yoga-ez-fitness-wear.com/yogastyles.html

[40] Gupta, 2007, op. cit., p. 83.

> Cry to your mother Shyama with a real cry, o mind! And how can she hold Herself from you? How can Shyama stay away? How can your mother Kali hold Herself away? O, mind lay at her feet your offering and with it mingle the fragrant sandal paste of love.[41]

If we go through *Gita* IX.26 we find how a true devotee attains God by love:

> Whosoever offers to me with love a leaf, a flower, a fruit or even water, I appear in person before that disinterested devotee of sinless mind, and delightfully partake of that article offered by him with love.

What Lord Krishna says in the above-mentioned verse can be understood well in the light of what Ramakrishna Paramahansa says in the following lines:

> God cannot be seen with these physical eyes. In the course of spiritual discipline one gets a "love body" endowed with "love eyes", "love ears", and so on. One sees God with these love eyes.[42]

But this is not possible without intense love for God. One sees nothing but God everywhere when one loves Him with great intensity. It is like a person with jaundice, who sees everything yellow. Then one feels, I am verily He.[43]

Thus we can say that supreme love manifests itself in various ways through the feelings, thoughts, conducts and actions of the devotee. He regards life as beautiful and worth living on account of this divine love. Gradually his whole nature changes and he feels as if he were losing his identity in his beloved God. Many lovers of God, however, preserve their individuality for the sake of worshipping him and serving His creatures; they are free nevertheless, from

---

[41] Gupta, 2007, op. cit., p. 83.

[42] Ibid., p. 84.

[43] Sardananda, 2003, *Sri Ram Krishna: The Great Master*, p. 115.

attachment to the world, for they realize that all things belong to the Lord. They love the universe because it is all His. This can be understood well if we see it in the light of what Yugrishi Shriram Sharma Acharya writes in his autobiography:

> The omnipotent God can only be *nirakara* (formless). God is known as *paramatma* which means that which includes and exceeds all living beings. It is *virat-brahma* or *virat-vishva.* Sri Krishna had shown a vision of this cosmic or universal God to Arjuna and Yashoda. Kaushalya and Kakbhushundi had also seen a glimpse of God in the form of entire universe. According to this conception the service to this *virat-brahma* is the service to God.[44]

Even Jesus Christ stated this ideal of *bhakti-yoga* when he taught: "As you have loved me, love one another".

We agree with Swami Vivekananda that the first angle of pure love is that it knows no bargaining. It is love for love's sake. The devotee loves God because He is lovable. The second angle is that supreme love knows no fear. A devotee does not love God for fear of punishment. As long as there is any fear in the heart there is no real love, for love conquers fear; they cannot coexist and the third angle is that love knows no rival; God is no longer sought in temples or churches, in heaven, or in the scriptures. There is no place where He does not exit.

Thus after a careful observation of the different paths of *yoga* it becomes very clear that they all lead to the same goal, that is self-realization. Roads are different but the destination is the same. It depends on the practitioner which path he chooses as per his temperament. Some may take one path as a key in order to experience self-realization, while others take another path, but the fact is that there is absolutely no difference between the various practices of *yoga*.

---

[44] Shriram Sharma, 2004, *My Life: Its Legacy and Message*, p. 97.

4

Importance and Applications of Yoga

THE need and importance of *yoga* can be understood well if we refer to the problems of the day and their solutions through *yoga*.

We are in the second decade of the twenty-first century. But there is a nagging question before us — have we really made progress? Are we living a happy and blissful life? The answer is almost "no" and "not at all"? In spite of the pace with which science has progressed — with new inventions in all walks of life, increased number of talented and intellectual people, revolution in the field of transport and communications — why is it that we are living such a miserable life? If this is progress, then why are we restless? Why do we see so many people committing suicides due to mental unrest? Why are students committing suicides due to ragging every year? Why is the number of people suffering from several mental diseases on the rise? Why are families getting broken with increased prosperity? Why indecency and sexual crimes are on the rise? Why is the crime rate on the rise? Why is the modern age is witnessing an increasing dilution of the moral fibre among the youth? Why are the rules of social conduct and the norms of behaviour developed by tradition breaking down? Why are we witnessing the rapid deterioration in moral values in all the spheres of life? Why are we becoming more and more Western and materialistic and running after transient chimeras of consumerism? Why are we witnessing communal and caste-based violence? Why are we witnessing scam after scam? Why is the corruption at its peak? Why is media losing its credibility? Why is media no longer a mission but a profession? Why are the electronic and print media overflooded with negative news? Can this be called progress?[1] These are some million dollar questions before us which have posed an alarming threat to the human society.

All these evils and problems show that the root cause of all the evils and agonies in the human society is ignorance. Just as the seed is the cause of the whole tree, *avidya* (ignorance) is the cause of all our miseries.[2] Therefore self-knowledge (*vidya*) is the only solution to these problems. This is the reason why our saints and seers stressed the importance of *yoga* in human life. Because it is through *yoga* that we can attain self-knowledge. Lord Krishna in *Gita* VI.23 says:

> *tam vidyad duhkha sanyoga viyogam yoga sanjnitam* ।
>
> *Yoga* is the destroyer of suffering.

Today, therefore, there is a need for *yoga* journalism to create awareness about *yoga* and spirituality among people for their well-being and holistic progress.

People, these days, are in need of inner peace and calmness and security, which can come only from self-knowledge and self-realization. The *yoga-sadhana* is needed not only for leading a successful worldly life but also for the attainment of the spiritual experience or the self-realization which is the ultimate goal of human life.

Thus keeping in view the challenges of the day and their solutions through *yoga* and spirituality, we can say that *yoga* can very effectively serve the individual, society and nation, in the following ways.

Developing a New Philosophy of Life and Yogic Lifestyle

Materialism and spirituality are the two ways of living. A man of materialistic lifestyle runs only after material possessions and

[1] *Akhand Jyoti*, January–February 2010, p. 5.

[2] Vivekananda, 2003, *Raja Yoga*, p. 171.

comforts.[3] The material possessions, for him, are the be-all and end-all of his life. He wants to get material possession by using every foul means and therefore creates problems for himself and the society. He goes on carrying the burden of miseries and agonies throughout his life.

Now that he has nothing to do with moral values. All his activities are against the interest of the society and humanity as well. On the other hand, a man who leads a spiritual lifestyle never uses foul means for the good of himself. He changes his thoughts, mode of living or his philosophy and view of life. Manifestation of inner consciousness is the goal of spiritual life. Another purpose of spiritual life is to eliminate all that is negative and evil in man's personality and to develop in him all that is sublime, good, auspicious and noble. This is done through the means of self-discipline and righteous living. Cultivation of positive traits such as purity, truthfulness, nobility, unselfish love, forbearance, absence of anger, greed and lust, spirit of brotherhood, self-sacrifice, integrity, composure of the mind and restraint of the senses form the various disciplines in spiritual life.

A spiritual man has an utmost desire to evolve himself ethically, morally and spiritually, and therefore he is no longer tormented by mental conflict, sorrow and suffering, and set upon a new vista of joyous experience and spiritual fulfilment.[4] Wherever he is, peace, prosperity and well-being follow him. Thus whatever problem, we witness today, is the result of materialistic vision of life, therefore spiritual lifestyle or its spiritual vision is the best philosophy of life and is the key solution to the problems of the day.

Pranav Pandya, the pioneer in scientific spirituality, has rightly remarked:

Value-based life, culture-based life, yogic or spiritual life is

---

[3] *Akhand Jyoti*, January–February 2003, p. 9.

[4] *Divine Life*, January 2003, p. 3.

> the only solution to all the problems that exist today. When this message of *yoga* and spirituality reaches not only the masses of our own nation but the entire world, fanaticism, terrorism, communal violence, naxalism, and corruption will automatically be wiped away.[5]

Ordinarily, an average person feels no need for a philosophy of life. He lives more by compulsion of circumstances created by his family, the neighbourhood and the group to which he belongs. Force of habit leads him to live his life as others live their lives. He feels no need for a change and therefore seldom thinks about a philosophy of life. Philosophy of life represents an objective and the principles as well as the ends and means. It is, in fact, a continuous process of living for an end, consciously decided upon by oneself. *Yoga* says that good ends do not justify bad means. For a clean philosophy of life both the ends and the means should be above board. A man with a philosophy of life, therefore is determined to apply the fair means to attain his ends. Another difference is that while an average man follows some philosophy, it is at the level of material life; but the *yoga*-oriented man lives at a higher level of serving humanity and has thus a moral-cum-spiritual end.[6] The yogic or spiritual philosophy of life is progressive so as to effect a man both externally at his behaviour pattern and internally at his basic attitude. Persons with no philosophy of life are forced to adjust to each and every demand and contingency. Such inconsistency involves much physical and mental wear and tear. Therefore a man without any philosophy of life is more or less like a vagrant whose life is just an accident, and he lives merely as a creation of habit and circumstances.

Unless man sets a goal and admits of a philosophy of life he can't progress, as he will lack stability. Sometimes men accept good ends but, when experiencing some difficulties, change to bad means and stoop to unsocial and immoral acts which lead only to suffering not only for themselves but also for others. Without a philosophy of

---

[5] *Akhand Jyoti*, September–October 2010, p. 7.

[6] Shri Yogendra, 1978, *Yoga Essays*, p. 55.

life and by resorting to bad means to achieve success, man invites ill health both of body and mind.

Yoga advises that a man must select his ends, draw his immediate objectives and principles, and apply the *yoga* means. It is absolutely necessary in life for a man to know what exactly he wants from life and how he would achieve it. Otherwise he will be like a ship without a helmsman that will be in trouble sooner or later and might even be wrecked.

A wavering mind, unprepared to accept any philosophy of life, merely drifts from day-to-day experiences with much sufferings and frustrations. On the death-bed, he knows that he has wasted away his life. But this last-moment realization does not help. It is the way of nature to take revenge on those who have no philosophy in contrast to those who achieve their ends and then die in peace.

In modern life the sense of duty has been reduced to mechanical functions without the spirit; lust for money has made man an exploiter, search for pleasure knows no limits and selfless life is a misnomer. The basic reason for all this is a wrong philosophy of life, and thus a man suffers because of himself; and the society, because of him.

Therefore there is the need of a sound philosophy of life for permanent peace and happiness in the life of an individual and society as well. People try to seek peace in alcohol, drugs and narcotics but philosophers have tried it with their philosophy. It is only *yoga,* which aims at an integrated man and integrated society, that can provide eternal peace and happiness, and thus solve the problems of humanity.

Thus *yoga*, as a philosophy of life, can play a pivotal role in motivating the masses to follow the moral values and spiritual lifestyle rather than the materialistic lifestyle, for a peaceful, pious, prosperous and blissful life.[7]

---

[7] Shri Yogendra, 1978, op. cit., pp. 50-51.

Yoga for Holistic Health

There goes the old adage:

> When wealth is lost, nothing is lost, when health is lost something is lost, when character is lost, all is lost.

Here the main emphasis has been laid on character, but the loss of health is also equally telling. It is a well-known fact that if we are healthy then we cherish various offerings of life better. We can also use all tools and resources at our disposal more effectively to achieve happiness.[8] Since ancient times sages have been saying: *sharir madhyam khalu dharma sadhanam,* implying that the body is the primary medium for practising *dharmas*. In the Indian context, every good and positive deed is about fulfilling one's *dharmas* (duties). Be it material or physical progress, nothing can be achieved without a healthy body.[9]

Swami Vivekananda rightly remarks:

> Be strong, my friends, that is my advice to you. You will be nearer to heaven through football than through the study of the *Gita*. These are bold words but I have to say them, for I love you. I know where the shoe pinches. I have gained a little experience. You will understand the *Gita* better with your biceps, your muscles, a little stronger.[10]

Thus the body is the medium through which we perform our duties, enjoy the pleasures of life and attain salvation as well. Therefore holistic health is the first need of life. Now the question arises: what is health? World Health Organization (WHO) defines health as a state of complete physical, mental and social well-being and not merely absence of disease. WHO has also in recent times suggested a fourth dimension: spiritual health.[11]

---

[8] *Akhand Jyoti*, July–August 2010, p. 40.

[9] Balkrishna, 2007, *Yoga in Synergy with Medical Science*, p. 11.

[10] *Complete Works of Swami Vivekananda*, vol. III, p. 242.

[11] www.indiadivine.org

The word *svasthya* (health) is translated as a person established in *sva* (self). Only that individual can be said to be completely *svastha* (healthy) who does not have any illness, who has overcome lust, greed, who has imbibed *adhyatma* (spirituality) in his lifestyle, who recognizes and fulfils his duties and who treats his body as a temple of God and exercises self-control.[12]

Thus we can say that a person can't be called healthy unless he possesses physical, mental and spiritual well-being. If the body is healthy and yet the person suffers from lust, anger, hatred, greed and other negative emotions, he becomes the victim of bad thoughts and deeds, then his body begins to deteriorate and spiritual progress also slows down.[13]

But are we really healthy? Can we think of five completely fit persons that we know? People who have no health problems whatsoever? No backache, no heart problems, no weight issues, no digestive disorders. How many did we count?[14] With the change in lifestyle came an increase in mental and physical disorders that are affecting people more vigorously. Today, anxiety, depression, stress, obesity, diabetes, cancer, acquired immune deficiency syndrome (AIDS), high blood pressure, heart diseases and respiratory problems are of epidemic scales. Cumulative research, media reports and anecdotal evidence over the past three decades reveal that suicides are an emerging epidemic the world over. Some 800,000 individuals in the world commit suicide every year largely on account of mental illness.[15]

According to the International Association of Suicide Prevention (IASP) more than a million people worldwide die by

---

[12] *Akhand Jyoti*, July–August 2010, p. 43.

[13] Balkrishna, 2007, op. cit., p. 13.

[14] *Times of India*, article "A Kick of Health", by Rutu Dutta, 30 April 2006.

[15] *Times of India*, article "Physician Heal Thyself", by Dileep Padgaonkar, 21 October 2009, p. 12.

suicide each year.[16] This phenomenon is growing in India too. It does not end here. Cancer is another malady. Every year 3 lakh people die due to this disease. India, according to a report of Cardiological Society of India, is also gradually becoming the hub of heart ailments. Unfortunately even after spending 60 thousand billion rupees on medical services only about 35 per cent of people, on falling sick, are able to control their disease under modern medical systems like allopathy, and about 65 per cent people, are not able to afford the allopathic treatment.[17] Modern medical science has been trying hard to find cure or control them but has not the desired results.

Thus the total burnout syndrome is quite a common phenomenon these days. So, what does one do to combat the unhealthy monster, which is hanging like a Sword of Damocles over head? The medical experts blame that the physical and mental disorders which we are witnessing these days are due to people's rapid transformation to an unhealthy lifestyle. In the last thirty years our lifestyle has changed dramatically. Thus we need to reverse this trend by adopting a holistic approach. This is where *yoga* opens its door.

Swami Ramdev very strongly remarks and recommends:

> The main factors of illness are tension, degrading immunity, pollution, degeneration of the internal organic system or the main parts and hereditary genes. *Yoga* prevents degeneration by strengthening the internal organic structure with the help of balanced diet. Healthy lifestyle and increasing immunity along with some yogic practices like *asanas* and *pranayamas* like *bhastrika*, *kapalabhati* and *anuloma-viloma*. We could achieve a state of complete health through yogic practices. Therefore *yoga* could be used not only as a philosophy but also as a weapon potent against physical and mental disorders. In

---

16 *Hindustan Times*, article "When Self Is the Enemy", by Satyem Mohapatra, 11 November 2009, p. 9.

17 Ramdev, 2009, *Jeevan Darshan*, p. 33.

> our society more than 100 crore people have benefitted from *yoga*. *Yoga* is now being accepted amongst doctors and scientists too, not just among common practitioners. It is the dawn of time when we should start accepting *yoga* or else our future generations might get entrapped in the endless epidemic cycles.[18]

Acharya Balkrishna remarks:

> From the very outset, *yoga* transforms the physical body. Self-discipline, celibacy, cleanliness and austere devotion, posture and *pranayama* have an important role in the transformation of the body. Practising *yoga* helps in keeping the gross and subtle organs active in its natural state. Needless to say that natural functioning of the body organs is the basis of good health. The health maintained through artificial means can't be lasting. Consuming medicines especially allopathic not only reduces the sensitivity of physical organs but also eliminates the chances of reinstating the natural processes. It so happens that in the process of curing one disease, a particular medicine causes another. But different yogic practices like *asanas*, *pranayamas*, *mudra*, *bandha*, *shatkarma* clean or refine different glands, blood, vital energy (*prana*) and other organs. All the waste matters that are the root cause of all disorders and diseases are eliminated from the body. The body which is maintained with proper diet, sleep and celibacy does not fall sick. The first two stages of *ashtanga-yoga*: *yama* and *niyama* actually forms the basis for a healthy human being and a healthy society.[19]

He further says:

> It is true that common man can't afford huge cost of medicines and treatment. Sixty-five per cent of Indian population and a large number of people in other countries who can't even think of seeking expensive medical treatment

[18] *Yoga Sandesh*, December 2010, p. 14.

[19] Balkrishna, 2007, op. cit., pp. 15-16.

> have been blessed with life-saving medicine in the form of *yoga*. It is also a blessing for those who are well off but are almost dead as they suffer from incurable diseases. They have the resources but don't know what treatment to take. *Yoga* has prevented people from getting into such dismal situations. *Yoga* offers recourse for those who have lost hope; it opens a new path when all other paths are closed.[20]

Today *yoga* has emerged as a therapy across the globe. Many scientific researches have shown the therapeutic impact of *yoga*. *Yoga* is being used as a therapy in various hospitals and clinics world over. The *yoga* therapy has been proved successful in the treatment of various physical and mental disorders. In fact, mental problems are the root cause of various health problems and therefore the mind and the spirit should be provided with some form of rejuvenation and stress relief.

The psychosomatic diseases cannot be uprooted only by treating the body. Since psychosomatic diseases are primarily a mental phenomenon, mere medical and surgical management does not give permanent solution to the problem; and there is absolutely no other satisfactory method to overcome these problems in the modern medical sciences. It is *yoga* which gives a permanent solution.[21]

The mind, body and spirit concept basically is based on the view that we human beings stand on three pillars: the thought process, which is the product of our mind, the physical expression of existence, which is our body, and our inner being, which is called the spirit. The human existence therefore needs the well-being of all these three pillars for holistic health. That is why now even the modern medical sciences have started focusing more on the holistic treatment of the individual rather than just giving treatment to the body.[22] Now that *yoga* simultaneously acts on physical, mental

---

[20] Balkrishna, 2007, op. cit., p. 56.

[21] *Yoga and Total Health*, July 2009, p. 7.

[22] www.articledoctor.com

and spiritual levels, it paves the way for the overall well-being of the individual.

On physical level, *yoga* helps in cleansing the internal organs of the body, i.e. blood vessels, cells, respiratory and digestive systems and makes the waste matter comes out of the body. *Yoga* also increases the immunity of the body and thus the body becomes capable of fighting against diseases. The tired, weary body becomes energetic; the person becomes active and gets a new direction with regular practice of *yoga*. On mental level, *yoga* increases mental power and destroys mental disorders. *Yoga* increases the concentration of mind. The improved concentration and clarity of mind enhances the skills and increases productivity. Several researches have shown that *yoga* helps to relax and handle stressful situations. *Yoga* instills a deep sense of well-being which has its inward focus teaching the mind to let go off negative thoughts and stress. *Yoga* thus encourages positive thoughts, quieten the mind so that one can focus on one's energy where he wants it to go.[23]

On emotional level, *yoga* refines the emotions of the individual. It is emotion or feeling which endows a person with human virtues. All the human virtues remain undeveloped and incomplete without emotion or feeling. If a person is emotionally weak, undeveloped or frustrated; he is deprived of pleasure and bliss. If such a person is emotionally hurt, his life becomes very painful. His life is totally destroyed or ruined. *Yoga* in fact is the technique of refining emotion. It purifies the heart and soul, washing away their dirt. A person, whose heart is pure, is free from mental and emotional disorders. A man, who is emotionally unstable, never gets pleasure and peace. He is deprived of human virtues like truth, love, sympathy, service, cooperation and affection. Those virtues can never manifest unless a man does *yoga* practices like *dharana*, *dhyana*, *upasana* and prayer. In modern times, when a person is flooded with negative emotions like cruelty, selfishness, hatred

[23] www.yogamovement.com

and jealousy the only option and solution left to get rid of them is *yoga*. On spiritual level *yoga* paves the way for the spiritual well-being of the individual.

To be spiritual means to be pious and compassionate. *Yoga* stops the fluctuations of the *chitta* (mind) and makes way for the union of individual consciousness with universal consciousness. This is what is called spiritual experience or the attainment of liberation which is the ultimate goal of *yoga*. If a man follows the path of *yoga* then he undoubtedly can attain this ultimate goal. A man no doubt wants to go ahead on the path of salvation (liberation) but the seeds of *karma*, the good or bad impressions of the *karma* as well as other factors sprung from ignorance come on his way as a barrier and stops him from proceeding ahead on this path. The individual soul thus, due to the impression of the *karma*s of the previous births remains unaware of his true self. But when the impressions (dirt) covering the individual soul is washed away and uprooted by the practice of *yoga*, the individual soul is introduced to its real form.

This is what Lord Krishna in *Gita* IV.37-38 says:

> As the blazing fire turns the fuel to ashes, Arjuna, even so the fire of knowledge turns all actions to ashes. On earth there is no purifier as great as knowledge. He who has attained purity of heart through a prolonged practice of *karma-yoga* automatically sees the light of truth in the self in course of time.

Thus, we see how *yoga* paves the way for physical, mental and spiritual well-being and provides the individual holistic health. The use of *yoga* as a therapy makes one completely healthy by uprooting the diseases. Another remarkable thing about this therapy is that it is very easily available and affordable to the common masses. It has no side-effects. Like other therapies, *yoga*, in fact, is a holistic approach which teaches a new lifestyle and way of thinking.

Needless to say that therapy is not the goal of *yoga*, rather the ultimate goal of *yoga* is self-realization. But how can a sick person attain self-realization without physical, mental and spiritual well-being. This is the reason why our seers, apart from propounding means for gaining self-realization such as meditation and *samadhi*, they developed a system for keeping people healthy and disease free through various yogic practices.

Seers, although not having material comforts, would yet live a blissful life. Why? Because *yoga* was the part and parcel of their lives. They had adopted *yoga* as a lifestyle.

Shedding light on the importance of *yoga* for a healthier and happier life, *Shvetashvatara Upanishad* 2.12 states:

> *na tasya rogo na jara na mrityuh, praptasya yogagnimayam shariram* II
>
> Having attained the *yogagnimaya sharira* one wins diseases, ageing (oldhood) and premature dealth as well. The exertion done in *yoga* practice never goes in vein as it kills all types of suffering.

Hatha-Yoga Pradipika states:

> *laghavam karma samartham sthairyam duhkha sahishnuta*
>
> From yogic practices there comes lightness and stability in the body and the body is free from pain and diseases.

At the same time there is an increase in the physical strength and stamina of the body. The pain-bearing capacity of the body increases as well.

Even *Gheranda Samhita* says:

> *na cha rogon na cha klesha arogyam cha dine dine* I
>
> A person, practising *yoga*, is oppressed neither by diseases nor by *kleshas* (pain) and attains holistic health day by day.

Thus considering the holistic approach of the *yoga* one must adopt it in one's life as a lifestyle for holistic health this is what Lord Krishna says in *Gita* VI.17:

> *yuktahar viharasya yuktacheshtasya karmasu* I

> *yuktasvapnava bodhasya yogo bhavati duhkha* ||
>
> *Yoga* is neither for him who overeats, nor for him who observes a complete fast; it is neither for him who takes too much sleep, nor even for him who is ceaselessly awake? *Yoga*, which rids one of woe, is accomplished only by him who is regulated in diet and recreation, regulated in sleep and wakefulness.

Thus this directly applies to us in our modern-day life. Lord Krishna advises us to lead our lives as a *yogi* and its principles should reflect in our diet, deeds, sleep and wakefulness.

Application of Yoga in the Field of Education

Sri Aurobindo says:

> The children should be helped to grow up into straightforward, frank, upright and honourable human being ready to develop into divine nature.

Yugrishi Shriram Sharma Acharya remarks:

> Education should mould students from top to bottom in such a way that they become true human beings.[24]

Swami Vivekananda says:

> The education which doesn't help the common mass of people to equip themselves for the struggle in life, which doesn't bring out strength of character, a spirit of philanthropy and the courage of a lion — is it worth the name?[25]

If we evaluate the present education system in the light of what these great men have said about education, can we say the education that is being imparted to our students is in accordance with the real sense of the term? And if it is not, then how can such a change in the education system be brought about to make education more

---

[24] *Akhand Jyoti*, January–February 2010, p. 26.

[25] *Complete Works of Swami Vivekananda*, vol. VIII, pp. 147-48.

relevant and pertinent in a rapidly changing world?[26]

If we look at the present education system we find that it is, of course, producing clerks, doctors, engineers, teachers, etc. But can we say that it is also producing good human beings? This is of course a million dollar question before us. Today crime, violence, indiscipline, disrespect for teachers, ragging, examination phobia seem to be very common among students and in educational institutes.

Moreover, even highly educated and intellectual persons are engaged in immoral activities. Why? Because they are deprived of moral values. Another ill effect of the present education system is rote learning. The dangers caused by this tendency of rote learning have been very beautifully depicted in the film *Three Idiots*.

This is what Swami Vivekananda says:

> Education is not the amount of information that is put into your brain and runs riot there, undigested all your life. We must have life-building, man-making, character-making assimilation of ideas. If you have assimilated five ideas and made them your life and character, you have more education than any man who has got by heart a whole library.[27]

Education must prepare us for life in the widest sense. It must help blossom the very best in an individual, the unique and exquisite something which every individual is born to offer to the world. It is here *yoga* opens its door because *yoga* in itself is a process of self-education, which helps in the evolution of an individual consciousness. However, it can be of enormous help in the present set-up of education for its utilitarian aspect. Today a child needs good memory, quick recollection, sharp intellect, quick decision-making power, a clear perception, keen observation, and high capacity to absorb and assimilate the heavy package of information

---

[26] www.narendramodi.in

[27] *Complete Works of Swami Vivekananda*, vol. III, p. 302.

and knowledge under the pressure and stress all around. A graded set of yogic practices can be of immense help if undertaken as a daily routine along with the adoption of yogic pattern of behaviour with due emphasis on moral values and outlook towards all living beings.[28]

We are constantly bombarded with messages from various sources about the benefits of *yoga*. Our children, students, the future of our society, also need to learn about the benefits of *yoga*. Their lives are burdened with activities and classes. They have to face high expectations of parents, educational insitutions, job providers, in addition to peer pressure. This leads to the accumulation of stress and tension, inability to focus and concentrate, and the development of different physical and mental disorders. How can *yoga* help? The importance of *yoga* education is that *yoga* can be used not just for releasing stress and improving body's functions, but also for developing the overall personality. It helps us move from paper and pencil, learning by rote system, job-oriented education to personal, experimental, life-building, man-making, character-making education.[29]

The purpose of yogic system of education is to awaken the inherent potentials of the individual. Several scientific researches reveal that yogic practices are useful for the awakening and evolution of inner potentials.

Emphasizing the importance of *yoga* education for students Swami Satyananda Saraswati says:

> We will have to transmit the knowledge in a symbolic form directly into the subconscious mind of the child. This is precisely the system of education in *yoga*. *Yoga* stresses on all aspects of life. *Yoga* helps the students to attain ethical perfection and perfect concentration of mind and to unfold

[28] Korpal and Shankar, 2005, *Hatha Yoga for Human Health*, p. 55.

[29] www.wellbeing.com

various psychic powers.[30]

This system of education in *yoga* can be understood well in the light of what Swami Satyananda Saraswati writes about his experiment with *yoga-nidra*:

> The principle of *yoga-nidra* can be applied for increasing knowledge. Teachers and parents should be able to communicate with the subconscious mind of the child. This communication can take place only if you know how to develop the child's subconscious state. I have tried many experiments with *yoga-nidra*. For example, in 1964, a child of four came to join me as a Swami. I could not accept him at such an early age, so I told him to come back when he was seven years old and then I would accept him. To my amazement, on the day he turned seven, the boy left his home and came back to me. This gave me an indication of his mental character. That boy lived with me for about eight years. Throughout this period he created unending problems and disturbances for me. All day long he used to break things and play tricks on the visitors who came to the *ashrama*, he was not prepared to go to school or to study anything. So what did I do? I experimented on him with *yoga-nidra*. As soon as he went to bed at night, I would note the time. Then after five minutes I would start reciting the *Gita*, the Upanishads, the Bible anything else that I wanted him to learn. This worked very well so I did another experiment. I tried reading to him in English and then in other languages. I finished my experiment within two years and today he is one of the most brilliant Swamis I have.[31]

Thus the above indicates how the education of a child can be imparted even without the child's knowledge. The brain composition has to be influenced by certain practical methods. Through the practice of *yoga-nidra*, *pranayama*, *surya-namaskara* and chanting of *mantra*, the inner components of the brain can be

---

[30] Saraswati, 2003b, *Yoga Education for Children*, pp. 16-17.

[31] Saraswati, 2003b, op. cit., p. 17.

brought to a point of regulation. It is said that only the 7-8 per cent part of the brain of even highly-educated persons is awakened, the rest part of the brain remains latent but *yoga* says that it can be awakened completely by yogic practices if it is practised since very childhood. On the basis of this very vision students did learning and *yoga* practice simultaneously in our ancient *gurukula* system. Consequently, bold, energetic, talented students were moulded. Students used to be good human beings. Through the practice of *yoga*, there comes the evolution of human virtues like truth, service, cooperation, harmony, benevolence, sacrifice, generosity and sympathy within the individual.

Thus we can say that an integrated education, based on the Indian yogic science, is aimed at the total and complete development of the individual endowed with; a strong, supple, well-formed and healthy body, a sensitive, unselfish and mature emotional nature, a positively energetic vital and enlightened mind, a wide-ranging and vibrant intelligence, a strong will, a balanced and pleasant personality, and the subtler spiritual qualities that can channellize, harmonize and direct an individual into a life that is beneficial to himself, his fellowmen, the society and the world as well.

Therefore *yoga* needs to be applied in the field of education. It is as relevant today as it was in ancient past. Today many schools, colleges, universities have added *yoga* to their curriculums but it needs to be applied across educational institutes on a large scale. We can say that it is essential that we understand the true meaning of spirituality and *yoga*, their importance and the role they have to play in education. Because without this understanding, we will continue to merely imitate, and that too poorly, some often discarded values and structures of a purely Western education and culture. And we may then be able to contribute more meaningfully to a greater perfection in the world also.

For the Promotion of Health Tourism

Tourism is an important source of income for developing nations like India. Today even in tourism industry, health tourism is developing very fast. More than half of the tourists come to India are for the purpose of pilgrimage and health care. For health tourists *yoga* and Ayurveda have become the focal point of attraction; as the traditions of *yoga* and Ayurveda are integrally related to India. There are various places which are becoming popular from the point of view of health tourism. On such places a large number of tourists undergo training in *yoga*, Ayurveda, Naturopathy, etc. It seems that today *yoga* has become a powerful tool for attracting the tourists. Hotels, resorts, etc. conduct *yoga* sessions as part of the tour package. Both tourists and businessmen benefit.[32]

Application of Yoga in Different Fields

Today *yoga* is being applied in different fields. Whether they be musicians, singers, players, policemen, media persons – they all can develop their working capacity and perform their action with excellence. As *Gita* II.50 says:

> *yogah karmashu kaushalam*
>
> Which implies that *yoga* is skill and excellence inaction.

Today many sports personalities of the world are practising *yoga* for better performance. Different sports teams of the world are taking the service of *yoga* trainers for better performance. Even management institutes and industrial houses are taking the service of *yoga* trainers for increasing the working efficiency and performance of their students and employees.[33]

Yoga is being adopted even by film actors and actresses for beauty and fitness. In the quest for a beautiful figure and overall fitness, *yoga* is one of the most sought-after techniques. "Beauty with *yoga*" is a reality since regular practice of *yoga* helps a woman remain agile and slim. *Pashchimottanasana*, *sarvangasana*, *halasana*,

---

[32] *Yoga Vijnana*, paper-1, 2009, Distance Education Program, DSVV, Haridwar, p. 16.

[33] Ibid., p. 14.

dhanurasana, virasana and *ardha-matsyendrasana* can help one sculpt one's body. Just by devoting about twenty minutes daily to *yoga* one can improve one's natural charm.[34] This is the reason why *yoga* is being adopted by film stars for beauty and fitness.

On the other hand, because of the application of *yoga* on large scale in different fields, it has today even emerged as a profession. Today government, semi-government, private institutions and universities in India and abroad run a number of certificate, diploma and degree courses in *yoga*. After passing out, many of them take up *yoga* as a profession of teaching at the school, college and university levels. Some *yoga* teachers are running their own centres to cure various diseases through *yoga*. Even in different hospitals and clinics the services of *yoga* therapists are available.[35]

Creating and Cultivating Spiritual Ambience in the Family

The family is the basic unit of the society, where an individual is shaped and nurtured. Creating a society of tolerant and caring individuals begins with family. Children when taught good values from the very beginning understand the importance of human dignity; they are disciplined and conscious of their rights and duties, ready to work hard and strive for excellence. Maintaining a congenial environment at home is conducive for building strong family bonds, which provide emotional sustenance. In a broader sense the whole world is one family – *vasudhaiva kutumbakam*. Love and understanding in families will promote harmonious societies, where we show concern and compassion for fellow human beings.[36]

Yugrishi Shriram Sharma Acharya says: "A family full of love and cooperation is a heaven on the earth."

In the light of these words it is up to us to think: is there any such heavenly atmosphere in a family today? The answer is almost

---

[34] www.target.com

[35] Korpal and Shankar, 2005, op. cit., p. 60.

[36] President of India.nic.in/sp130810.html

in the negative. Why? Because there seems to be no such love, affection, faith, sacrifice, truth, mutual respect and understanding among the family members – which make a family a heaven.

Brothers like Rama, Bharat, mothers like Kaushalya, Madalasa, Anusuya, mothers-in-law like Kaushalya, fathers-in-law like Dashrath, and sons like Rama and Shravan Kumar are rarely found in the family today. The true picture of most of the families of the day has been very beautifully presented in the film *Baghban*. The story of this film is, in fact, the true story of most of the families.

How can a family be like a heaven when each and every member of the family is deprived of human values like truth, love, compassion and sacrifice? Under such conditions, therefore, it is *yoga* which, if practised by family members, can pave the way for heavenly atmosphere in the family. Because it is *yoga* which inculcate divine virtues like love, truth, faith, sacrifice, cooperation in a person. The *yama* and *niyama* (non-violence, truth, non-stealing, celibacy, non-possessiveness, cleanliness, contentment, austerity, self-study and devotion to God) as has been prescribed by Maharshi Patanjali in his *Yogasutra*, of course, enrich and enlighten the family life with divine virtues/*sanskara*. Spiritual lifestyle creates spiritual ambience and heavenly atmosphere in the family. And in such a spiritual ambience, there is the possibility of personality development of a man who, then of course, can contribute to the society and nation building as well.

Now let us have a glance at the heavenly atmosphere in a family. Here in these lines from *Ramacharitmanas*, Balakanda 204.4 we can see the ideal lifestyle and heavenly atmosphere in the family:

> *pratkal uthi kai raghunatha* । *matu pita guru navahin matha* ।।
> *ayasu magi karahin pur kaja* । *dekhi charit harshai man raja* ।।
>
> The lord of Raghus would get up early in the morning and after bowing his head to his parents and preceptor, and taking their permission, would busy himself with the affairs of the city? The king was glad at heart to see his way of life.

The father-in-law's love for his daughters-in-law can be seen in *Ramacharitmanas,* Balakanda 354.4:

> *badhu larikanin par ghar ayin* । *rakhehu nayan palak ki nai* ।।
>
> King Dashrath then summoned the queens and showing every honour to them all admonished them in gentle tones: "The brides are still children and have come to a strange house; take care of them as eyelids that take care of the eyes."

Now we can see mothers-in-law's love for daughters-in-law's in *Ramacharitmanas,* Balakanda 357.2:

> *sundar bahunha sasu lai soyin* । *phanikanha janu sirmani goyin* ।।
>
> Mothers-in-law then slept with the lovely brides enfolded in their arms, like serpents that have clasped to their bosoms the precious jewel from inside their heads.

Now we just see true love of brothers for each other in the following lines from Ayodhyakanda 259.4 where Bharat recalls how Rama would love him in so many ways:

> From my infancy I have never left his company, and at no time has he hurt my feelings. I have experienced in my heart my lord's gracious ways, for even when I was losing in a game he would allow me to win.

On the other hand, Rama expresses his love and sacrifice for Bharat in the following lines form Ayodhyakanda 41.1:

> *bharatu pranpriya pavahin raju* । *bidhi sab vidhi mohi sanmukh aju* ।।
>
> Again Bharat, who is dear to me as my own life, will get the sovereignty; God is altogether propitious to me today.

Such a family is in fact a heaven on the earth but such heavenly atmosphere in the family can be created only by the practice of *yoga*. As the great Yugrishi Shriram Sharma Acharya says:

> *Grihastha* (householder) is a *tapovana* (a place for performing austerities) where one has to exercise the

spiritual disciplines like restraint, service and tolerance.[37]

Today most of the families lead a broken life with issues like wife-beating, bride-burning for dowry, murder of parents for a piece of land, etc. For these social issues *yoga* is the only remedy. *Yoga* can play a major role in creating spiritual ambience for a happier and ideal family life.

Yoga for Social Transformation

No doubt, the ultimate goal of *yoga* is self-realization but *yoga* at the same time paves the way for physical, mental, spiritual and social well-being as well. While *yoga* gives immense benefits to the body, mind and spirit of the individual, society gets transformed into a healthy, harmonious, prosperous, peaceful and blissful one.

The *yoga* makes one aware of his own true nature, the inner self; so that one can see oneself in pristine clarity. Once we have a glimpse of our true nature: who are we? Then the whole world changes. Because the change always begins with oneself. As Swami Vivekananda says: "Be and make". Even Mahatma Gandhi used to say: "If you want change, be a change first". Therefore the transformation of the society will happen only with the transformation of the individual. Therefore only a person who is aware of his inner self can be a part of social change or social transformation.[38]

Needless to say that for a healthy and beautiful society, energetic and active human beings are necessary. *Yoga* is therefore applicable not only in the personal life but in the social life as well. A person is the smallest unit of the society, therefore when an individual is shaped and nurtured with human values through the practice of *yoga*, a society of tolerant, truthful, non-violent, unselfish, honest and caring individuals begins to build up from that very moment.

---

[37] Shriram Sharma, 1998a, *Vangamaya: Grihastha ek Tapovana*, p. 1.

[38] Vivekananda, 2000, *Six Lessons on Raja-Yoga*, p. 7.

Yoga employs a broader holistic approach that focuses on teaching people a new lifestyle, way of thinking and way of being in the world. The role of *yoga* for healthy and happy living has been recognized even by scientists all over the world. So, for creating a beautiful and harmonious society *yoga* is the idle way.[39] *Yoga* establishes harmony between mind, body and soul. A person who does not possess physical, mental, spiritual and social well-being, is a danger for himself and society as well. Today the current society is overflooded with evil tendencies like violence, crime, corruption, selfishness and countless immoral and inhuman activities. Why? Because a person living in society is not mentally, spiritually and socially healthy. He is deprived of moral values. He lacks clarity, and understanding to act. So he is baffled and confused. It is where *yoga* opens its door to help us. As *Gita* II.50 says:

> *yogah karmashu kaushalam*
>
> Skill in action lies in *yoga* or the excellence in action is *yoga*.

To lessen the moral evils and crimes in the society, men in power and position should present a good example by leading moral lives and by being fair and just in their dealings — this is why *Gita* lays great emphasis on *lokasangraha* (welfare of humanity) *nishkama karma*, i.e. doing one's duty selflessly without thinking of any immediate or remote gain for himself, and *samatva* — fairness, justice and equality and interest in the good of all creatures, etc. The *yoga* can be practised even by ordinary people, in order to have every chance to atain a higher level of consciousness, the fountainhead of automatic ethical values and abode of bliss.

The *yoga* very scientifically begins with the emphasis on values through *yama* and *niyama*. *Yama*: non-violence, truthfulness, non-stealing, celibacy, non-possessiveness, and *niyama*: cleanliness, contentment, austerity, self-study and devotion to God actually form the basis for a healthy human being and a healthy society. Maharshi Patanjali calls *yama* having universal significance

---

[39] Balkrishna, 2007, Souvenir, p. 13.

and universal application. For social transformation a major transformation is required in our thinking process. The *yama* and *niyama*, in fact, constitute the foundation for one's thoughts, beliefs, attitudes, habits and actions. *Yama* is basically concerned with the social behaviour of an individual. It underlines the social code of conducts for an individual, whereas *niyama* underlines the personal code of conduct for an individual. *Yama* and *niyama*, on the one hand regulates one's behaviour, and on the other hand their practice change the society as well. Even the practice of truthfulness and non-violence has great power to change the society. Through *yoga* man can balance his emotions and become useful to himself and society. *Yoga* helps in balancing the emotions and changes the social perception of an individual. Today persons violating personal and social code of conducts are involved in various self-centred behaviour. They are basically concerned with their own selfish ends. The result is what we are witnessing social evils everywhere like corruption, cheating, violence, terrorism, naxalism, rape and sexual harassment. Our media are overflooded with such news and views. The application of *yama* and *niyama* can play a major role in eradicating these social evils.[40] They can lead to motivation and commitment for decisions to devote oneself for the welfare and transformation of the individual and society as well. The healthy and transformed society, in turn, will build up healthy individuals without any discrimination of caste, creed, colours, etc. The individual and society are complementary and supplementary to each other. One influences the other, one can't do without the other.

Therefore, a desirable level of personal and ethical values help to purify social evils and to transform society for mutual welfare where there is no exploitation, corruption and violence and each and every mind is pure and fear free. An individual is constantly engaged in examining one's values. One always bears in mind that moral values bring peace, integrity, contentment and bliss; while immoral values bring confusion, conflicts and unhappiness. One

[40] Balkrishna, 2007, op. cit., p. 157.

comes to know that one can choose one's values for a blissful life. Responsible and right actions stem out of the adoption of right values and thoughts. Thus values are the core of a worthy individual and desirable social set-up. Values are our invisible governors.[41] Mahatma Gandhi has very rightly remarked in this regard:

> In order to bring about social change we have to channellize human values through education. Truth and non-violence can generate human values. Moreover they are fully capable of guiding people today if they are applied accordingly and will continue to do so in the future.

Gandhiji emphasized the adoption of *ahimsa* (non-violence), which is eternal, natural and supreme in terms of human value. For Gandhi, non-violence is an active, pure means and has an all-time value. It is the best means to reach the truth.[42] It is a well-known fact that only with his commitment to truth and non-violence Gandhiji succeeded in bringing about a major change in the society.

Yugrishi Shriram Sharma Acharya very beautifully stresses the need of human values for social transformation:

> Evil actions are the root cause of the sufferings in the world. Therefore all the evil actions will have to be demolished. And the only option left to demolish the evil actions is the inculcation of values, idealism in the life of an individual. As the evil actions result from evil thoughts, evil actions can be destroyed only by good thoughts.
>
> A person with good thoughts is always careful about the good and bad consequences, and impact of his actions on the society. Such a person believes that God dwells in his heart and he sees whatever good or bad he does. He is fearful of the evil consequences of the evil action; therefore he never deviates from right actions. He is never involved in immoral activities and therefore brings peace, progress and welfare for both the individual and the society as well.

---

41 Balkrishna, 2007, op. cit., p. 151.

42 www.mkgandhi-sarvodaya.org/articles/sept 0802.html

> Therefore good thought is the basis of a healthy and transformed society. But what is the way of creating good thoughts? It is spiritualism. The spiritualism, the basis of which is benevolence, unselfishness and doing good to others. The more benevolent and unselfish a man will be, he will have the *darshan* of his own soul in others. Indifferent to sensual objects, storehouses of amiability and other virtues, grieving when they see others in distress and rejoicing at the sight of others joy, even minded and looking upon none as their enemy, free from vanity and passion; such people are the conquerors of greed, intolerance, exultation and fear. They are abodes of peace, dispassion, humility and joy. In their hearts dwell all such noble qualities as placidity, guilelessness and friendliness.
>
> Therefore the dream of the transformation of the society can come true only by banning the evil actions by purifying one's thoughts with spirituality.[43]
>
> *Yoga* not only liberates the soul but transforms the whole personality and therefore man becomes more humane, kind and useful for the society.[44]

Therefore, the application of *yoga* for social well-being and social transformation is the need of the hour. When the sun of *yoga* will shine over the horizon of the world and society today, the social evils, all the immoral and inhuman behaviour will disappear and the dream of a peaceful, prosperous, blissful and transformed society will be fulfilled. *Yoga* indeed immerses a person into the essence of *satyam-shivam-sundaram* and therefore the society having such persons is like a heaven on the earth.

Yoga for Nation Building

Today we are witnessing several national calamities/crises due to the degradation of personal and national character. They are

---

[43] Shriram Sharma, 1998d, *Vangamaya: Samajik, Naitik Evam Bauddhik Kranti Kaise?*, pp. 7.8-9.

[44] Balkrishna, 2007, op. cit., p. 169.

crimes, corruption, criminalization of politics, violence, religious fundamentalism, disharmony, vote-bank politics, etc.

But the remedy of all these national maladies is *yoga*. Because, when a person will return to his self through *yoga*, the centre of his soul, he will become incapable of any anti-self-conduct. Soul is pure and sacred by its very nature. Soul is replete with love, compassion, luminosity, radiance, peace, truth, consciousness and bliss.[45]

Therefore a person situated in his soul has a deep feeling inside that his body is constituted by the food, water and air. He feels that each cell of his body is made with the soil of his country. When such a person starts harbouring such sentiments, he can never betray his country. He will feel like betraying himself if he thinks of betraying his country. How can he be a traitor? He will love his county and the countrymen. It is the only solution to the social evils.

Swami Ramdev remarks:

> It is therefore my firm belief that only through *yoga* and spiritualism the personal and national character can be built. Sensitivity in place of insensitivity, trust in place of distrust, hope in place of despair and a sense of self-pride in the country in place of self-deprecation can be brought about. And Bharat shall become a superpower of the world by regaining its lost glory.[46]

He further says:

> We intend to inculcate *yoga* culture in each individual and awaken in him the sentiments of nationalism. We want to use the power of *yoga* for stirring up feelings of patriotism in everybody. Every morning we want to elevate ourselves spiritually through *yoga* and devote our whole energy to the progress of our nation. We want the sacred mission of national awakening, through spiritual awakening by *yoga*, to move forward. Some persons are

---

[45] Ramdev, 2009, op. cit., pp. 39-40.

[46] Ibid., p. 40.

> inclined to ask: what is the relation between *yoga* and the development of the country? We want to make it clear that the development of the nation (or the nation building) without spiritual development (evolution) is merely a dream. Therefore, every morning we will do *yoga* for our spiritual development, and then during the whole day we will devote ourselves to the development of prosperity of our nation. *Yoga* culture and nationalism are not opposite ideologies; they are rather complementary to each other.[47]
>
> A fully spiritual person can be free from corruption, crime, casteism and fanaticism. One who has realized his true "I" beyond the body and mind, and has perceived the extension of his "I" himself can't deceive others. He cannot be an accomplice in cases of bribery, theft, dacoity, murder and other crimes. Only *yoga* and spiritualism is the solution of the burning problems of an individual and the country.[48]

Swami Vivekananda says:

> India will be raised, not with the power of flesh, but with the power of spirit, not with the flag of destruction but with the power of peace and love.[49]
>
> Hidden under the ashes of apparent death, the fire of our national life is yet smouldering and that the life of this nation is spirituality. And your politics, society, municipality, plague-prevention work, and famine-relief work – all these things will be done as they have been done all along here, viz. only through spirituality; otherwise all your frantic yelling and bewailing will end in nothing, my friend.[50]
>
> The national ideals of India are renunciation and service. Intensify her in those channels, and the rest will take care

---

[47] Ramdev, 2009, op. cit., p. 20.

[48] Ibid., p. 105.

[49] *Complete Works of Swami Vivekananda*, vol. IV, pp. 352-53.

[50] Ibid., vol. V, p. 461.

of itself.[51]

Yugrishi Shriram Sharma Acharya strongly emphazises the role of spirituality in nation building:

> Citizens are the real national asset. Their emotional excellence as well as their excellence in action will make the nation prosper and progress by leaps and bounds. Even a nation of huge army, huge population, huge area and enormous resources will remain lying in distress and critical condition, if its citizens don't possess excellence in emotion and action. In earlier times even without enormous physical resources people would lead a more peaceful and blissful life, due to purity in their lives, but today despite having enormous physical resources we are not happy. People are behaving like wolf hungry and thirsty for one another's blood. Therefore unless our inner being will get purified, neither our thinking nor our action will be of any use to us and the nation. And unless our action is superior, our nation will not prosper.[52]

Thus by "cleaning inside through *yoga*, clean outside" — this principle has immense relevance for individuals, society, nations, politics, governance and mass media, where selfishness, indifference, and lack of purpose, commitment, service-orientation and accountability abound. These institutions have failed to inspire the people, because the leading personalities in them neither convey nor embody the message of inner transformation. Unwilling to banish the darkness within, they can hardly be expected to light the path of society and nation's progress.[53]

Here I see a great opportunity in journalism as a stakeholder of social changes and development. By spreading the message of *yoga* and spirituality, the media can destroy the darkness inherent

[51] Ibid., vol. V, pp. 227-28.

[52] Shriram Sharma, 1998d, op. cit., p. 7.11.

[53] *Indian Express*, article "Clean Inside, Clean Outside", by Sudheendra Kulkarni, 2 May 2010, p. 9.

within the individual, society and nation.

In fact, *yoga* is not of doing some aerobics or any other physical exercises as in a gymnasium. *Yoga* is a system which, if adopted, can lead to the control of mind, body and soul. It encompasses every aspect of human life, shapes our character and enables the mind to follow the path of wisdom, truth, humanity, love, sacrifice, non-violence and spirituality. Today, the practice of *yoga* has become a must and compulsory for everybody. Greed, jealousy, lust, anger, selfishness, laziness and other evils are dominating many people worldwide. Our society, per se, nation, is getting more and more insecure and uncomfortable due to criminalization of politics, violence, robberies, economic offences, religious fundamentalism and disharmony, threatening national integration. Excessive consumerism is putting strains on the natural resources, damaging our environment.

By following the path of *yoga* and spirituality everyone can improve the quality of his life and with such a change, many personal, social and national problems will automatically come down or disappear.

Yoga for Global Transformation

Talking of global Indian heritage, *yoga* is perhaps the most recognized one, having travelled all over the world for everyone's well-being. *Yoga,* like many cultural things, is a legacy of an ancient and continuous 5,000-years old Indian civilization and yet quite modern with the backing of science. The genesis of the globalization of *yoga* started in the West during the times of Plato and Aristotle who paid acknowledgements to Indian values and practices in their arts. These contacts were furthered by Alexander's arrival in India in the third century BCE. Modern *yoga* gained momentum since the second half of the nineteenth century due to the efforts of Swami Vivekananda and other great *gurus* like Osho, Maharshi Mahesh Yogi, Paramahansa Yogananda, Swami Satyananda, Shri Shri Ravi Shankar, Swami Ramdev, Pranav Pandya and many others, who travelled to the West and introduced the science and practice of *yoga.* And today *yoga*'s reach is very widespread. *Yoga* is now a multi-billion dollar industry in the world.

In the countries like United Kingdom, USA, France, Germany, Australia, the number of *yoga* practitioners is increasing everyday. This increasing influence of *yoga* in the West has made Christian evangelists so paranoid that they are demanding a ban on *yoga.* But still *yoga* is sweeping the world. The global celebration of *yoga* on International Day of Yoga on 21 June since 2015 is creating a new record of popularity every year. In India, Swami Ramdev is particularly well known for his efforts in popularizing *yoga* to the masses using mainstream media, claiming to have over 85 million people following his *yoga* camps via TV channels and video. This is in addition to some incredible work done by dedicated *yoga* centres like the Bihar School of Yoga, Shivananda Yoga Vedanta Centre, Dev Sanskriti Vishvavidyalaya, Gayatrikunj-Shantikunj and others.

Despite this explosion of *yoga*, can *yoga* be seen through narrow religious prisms? Is it fair when Christian extremists in the US and Islamic fundamentalists elsewhere demand its propagation and practice be banned among non-Hindus? Many orthodox Christian leaders have said that practising *yoga* is incompatible with teachings of Jesus. Muslim clerics have banned Muslims from practising *yoga* in Egypt, Malaysia and Indonesia, citing similar concerns.[54]

It is therefore the duty of the mass media that they project *yoga* in its real form to remove the misconceptions of the world humanity about *yoga.* We may have differences of opinion and factional disputes but *yoga* was given by the *rishi*s for the human race, not only for the Hindus. *Yoga* is not a religion but a science, a way of living. That is why *yoga* is called *sarvabhauma* (universal).

Yoga is in fact the technique of uniting the individual consciousness with universal or supreme consciousness. *Yoga* doesn't belong to any particular, caste, creed and religion. It is

---

[54] *Uday India* (Eng.), 13 November 2010, p. 50.

universal in appeal and therefore it belong to the whole humanity.

Yoga works on one's body, mind and soul. Therefore it is known as the global art. When our body, mind and soul are healthy and harmonious, we will bring health and harmony to the world — not by withdrawing from the world but by being a healthy living organ of the body of humanity. Therefore *yoga* is for the whole world and humanity.

If someone argues that *yoga* is only for some particular religion, he should be asked: is there a British cancer, an Italian cancer, or cancer one?[55]

Osho Rajnish very strongly argues in this regard:

> *Yoga* doesn't mean any kind of religious fanaticism. *Yoga* is spiritual in its nature and character. And spirituality does not mean that you have to preach Christianity, Hinduism, Islam or Jainism. Spirituality simply means spreading the basic fundamentals of all religions, which are all the same. Can love be Christian or Hindu? Can a peaceful mind be Hindu or Buddhist? Does a man of compassion have to be a Christian or a Jew?[56]

Pranav Pandya remarks:

> *Yoga* does not prescribe the worship of any specific "deity or deities". *Yoga* does not give specific instructions for the existence, nature or worship. *Yoga* is a universal science that has risen above religion. It has universal techniques. No particular dogma is laid down, and no particular God is pointed out for your worship. *Yoga* does not say that you must repeat any particular name of God. *Yoga* only says that repetition of one of the divine name is one of the ways of concentrating the mind. It does not specify the name or whom to worship.[57]

---

[55] Iyengar, 2000, *The Tree of Yoga*, p. 12.

[56] www.jadelotus.org/articles.htm

[57] *Uday India* (Eng.), 13 November 2010, p. 55.

H.R. Nagendra states:

> *Yoga* is a science of holistic living. It is Universal in its approach and applicable to all human beings irrespective of sex, age, caste, creed or religion. Anyone who wants to raise himself from the lowest level to the highest level of human achievement can take to *yoga.*[58]

Hrudananda Ray says:

> *Yoga* as a science of reunion can work and is working, fostering the well-being of a complete man. So simply it is a human science devoted to serve humanity beyond faith, belief and way of worship.[59]

Human sufferings are the same whether they are Hindus, Muslims, Christians, Jews or others. Whether they be Indian, Italians, Britishers or Americans. Everyone needs physical, mental and spiritual well-being for a peaceful, prosperous and blissful life. And *yoga,* in fact, serves this purpose. Afflictions of the body are the same. Afflictions of mind are the same. Diseases and sufferings know no caste, religion or nationality and *yoga* is given to cure those diseases. Nowhere in the ancient text is it said that *yoga* is only to be practised by the Hindus. On the contrary, Maharshi Patanjali describes *yoga* as *sarvabhauma.*

Maharshi Patanjali in *Yogasutra* 2.31 says:

> *jati desh kala samaya na vachchhinnah sarvabhauma mahavratam* ।
>
> When practised universally without exception due to birth, place, time and circumstances they (*yamas*) become great disciplines.

It is recommended that, they (*yamas*) should be practised universally without exception. There should be no modification due to differences in country, birth, time, place and circumstances.

---

[58] *Uday India* (Eng.), 13 November 2010, p. 59.

[59] Ibid., p. 63.

Thus *yoga* is a universal culture or it has a universal appeal. Just as it works on the whole of the individual, so it is meant for the development of the whole of mankind on the physical, mental and spiritual levels.

Today on global level we are witnessing several problems like terrorism, religious fanaticism, racial prejudices and hatred, ill policies and plans of the governments across the world. It is *yoga* which can give permanent remedies to these global problems.

Swami Shivananda remarks:

> In this age of atomic armament, racial hatred and policies of national greed, intolerance and distrust, our task is not so much the alteration and transformation of the patterns, policies and plans of the government of the nations of the world. The paramount importance and the imperative and indispensable necessity for the moral, ethical and cultural refinement of the individual personality upon a worldwide scale is to be realized first and foremost.
>
> For, the prime and fundamental unit of all wider groups like class, race, nation and human society the world over is the individual man. This is not an impossible proposition, for the divine exists in all beings and it is an integral part of every individual consciousness. The method to draw it out is right and true *yoga* or spiritual education.[60]

Yugrishi Shriram Sharma Acharya strongly recommends:

> The dream of the creation of a sinless society for the universal peace, prosperity and bliss can come true only when the ever happening evil deeds be totally banned by refining the thoughts through spirituality, otherwise there seems to be no other way of permanent and real peace and bliss in the world.[61]

Maharshi Aurobindo in his *Yoga and Its Objects* (p. 1), very beautifully

---

[60] *Divine Life*, August 2004, p. 3.

[61] Shriram Sharma, 1998d, op. cit., p. 7.9.

remarks:

> The *yoga* we practise is not for ourselves alone, its aim is to work out the will of the divine in the world, to effect a spiritual transformation and to bring down a divine nature and a divine life into the mental vital and physical nature and life of humanity. Its object is not personal *mukti*, although *mukti* is a necessary condition of the *yoga*, but the liberation and transformation of the whole human being.

Swami Ramdev argues:

> All persons in the world want peace and happiness. All the nations of the world agree on this point that peace should be established in the world. All people have some views about it according to their thinking capacity, but no unanimous solution is coming forth.
>
> Can there be some rules, values and norms which may be acceptable to all the people in the world, which do not trample upon the unity and integrity of an individual or the nation, which do not serve the personal vested interests of anybody, which any individual can, adopt, and achieve complete happiness, peace and bliss in life? It should be a path which every person can follow in the world fearlessly, with full freedom, and can achieve complete happiness, peace and bliss in life. This is the path of *ashtanga-yoga* propounded by the great sage Patanjali. This is not a creed, belief or sect; it is a complete method of living life. If the people all over the world are really serious about it that peace must be established in the world, its only solution is observance of *ashtanga-yoga*. It is only through eight-limbed (*ashtanga*) *yoga* that personal and social harmony, physical health, mental peace and spiritual bliss can be realized.
>
> The eight-limbed *yoga* passes the test of religion, spirituality, humanity and science. If the bloody strife in the world can be prevented by any means, it is *ashtanga-yoga* only. *Ashtanga-yoga* encompasses in a unique way the most sublime states of spirituality, right from general activities

to *dhyana* (meditation) and *samadhi* (self-absorption).[62]

In fact, one who treats universal and scientific values, ideals and traditions as a religion is a theist, a religious person, but not a fanatic. One who sees the image of God in all the creatures, including man and all the animate–inanimate objects, and allays the pain and misery in the world by dedicating his whole life to the service of all creatures, is a spiritualist. One who rises above all narrow-mindedness and loves mankind, and looks at the whole world like family from the depth of his heart — *vasudhaiva kutumbakam* (*Panchatantra* 5.38) — is a spiritualist.

This is what *yoga* teaches us. Spiritualism and nationalism are not mutually contradictory ideologies, but for the full freedom and security of every country and its citizens they are equally necessary. We are the citizens of an independent country, and it is our national moral responsibility to defend the independence, unity, integrity and sovereignty of the country. At the same time we are all one and are the children of one and the same God. Therefore, from the point of view of being God's children, according to the dispensation of that Supreme Lord, we are all brothers and sisters. This is what *yoga* teaches us.[63]

Today, the atmosphere of uncertainty, distrust and fear caused due to terrorism and religious hatred could be dealt with only by adopting and following the age-old philosophy of *yoga*, and thus there will be peace, bliss and prosperity in the world. Considering the universal application of *yoga*, we can say that *yoga* is the need of the day. The message of *yoga* needs to be spread fast in the world. Here journalism can play a crucial role in ensuring role in *yoga*'s spead across the globe.

Thus *yoga* and spirituality, having potentials for global transformation, can play a substantial role in making the individual, family, society, nation and the world more civilized, sophisticated

[62] Ramdev, 2009, op. cit., pp. 107-08.

[63] Ibid., p. 21.

and enlightened. Thus in this way the world we live in could be transformed into a better place.

For the Promotion of Positive and Healthy Journalism

Yoga and spiritual dimension introduced to journalism can promote a positive and healthy journalism. The functions of journalism are not just limited to disseminating information and entertaining the masses, rather it holds a greater responsibility. This is the reason why it is called the watchdog of the society and the fourth-pillar of democracy. The true function of journalism is to educate the public mind and not to fill the public mind with wanted and unwanted impressions. It is not the journalist's job to print news only, but to print what is fit to be printed in the greater interest of the individual, the society and the nation.

Needless to say that the media is a great power. It can effectively help in the formation of public opinion and can play a substantial role in making the individual, society and the nation more civilized, sophisticated and enlightened. But it is equally true that just as an unchained torrent of water submerges whole countryside and devastates crops, an uncontrolled media serves but to destroy. It can be profitable only when exercised from within. If this line of reasoning is correct, would journalism of the day stand the test?[64] How many press and TV channels would stand the test?

Be it the print or electronic media, all are flooded with negative news and views like crime, murder, violence, vulgarity, sensation, corruption, obscenity and what not which have negative impact on the readers and viewers? Is not even a single divine deed taking place on the earth or in the whole universe? But unfortunately the press and TV channels mostly cater to the lower taste of the readers and viewers, creating sensation, rather than educating and enlightening them for better citizenship and better human beings. It is really a short-cut to financial gains. It is always easier

---

[64] Gandhi, 2001, *An Autobiography*, p. 287.

to appeal to the lower passions of persons than to serve the real aim of journalism, i.e. service. We have heard media persons say "the people have to be given what they want". Any prostitute could also say the same thing. Can public be served even poison on this ground?

No doubt, journalism that gained name and fame because of its role in the freedom struggle of India has now taken a new turn. There has been a shift in the values and agendas of the press since the advent of globalization, privatization and liberalization, the focus being on market realities and market success. Most of today's print and electronic media owners or controllers are more concerned with the co-modification of their respective medium by treating news, views, events, advertisements, programmes and publicity as saleable commodities with scant regard for journalistic ethics and integrity. That journalism is essentially a service to the society has been vitiated by profit-oriented-business-soaked journalism. Journalism's first and foremost duty is to find out those truths which are in greater interest of the society. But now it is associated with sensationalism, exaggeration of unimportant facts and even manufactured truth.

The news and views which are advertisement-friendly are prominently published. Crimes and terrorism as well as other cruel and inhuman activities are being repeatedly broadcast or printed and this trend is on the increase. Celebrities and models are being projected as the icons of the society. The private lives of the so-called celebrities are given undue importance, sometimes neglecting crucial issues. How does it matter if two actors are having a feud between them? How does it matter if an actor is having an affair with someone? Somebody steals or rapes, what is the point of reporting it? Why make it a news unnecessarily to fill the space? All said, today, the journalism has become a puppet in the hands of a few capitalists and industrialists, and they are running channels and media houses as they run any other factory, therefore most of what we read and view in newspapers and channels are the products of such factories.

This situation is beautifully summarized in a pithy saying:

> If you do not read the newspapers, you are uninformed. If you do read the newspapers, you are misinformed.[65]

Therefore, today when journalism is suffering from several serious ailments like commercialism, sensationalism, corruption and populism, the fourth pillar of democracy itself, is in need of a pillar, the watchdog of the society itself needs to be watched for its own ethical code, a new dimension needs to be added to all forms of journalism, i.e. a spiritual dimension. Though it is happening at a miniscule scale in a few media houses, we have to go miles to make our media — print and electronic — to give them a spiritual dimension/direction. The need and importance of *yoga* journalism can be understood well in the light of what Osho says:

> Scanning the media, newspapers and listening to the news, both locally and globally, have not made you ever felt that something is seriously lacking? Something is missing? A new dimension needs to be added to all forms of journalism, the spiritual dimension — a positive message about the celebration of life. Spiritual journalism is happening on a small but expanding scale throughout the West, and if we could also integrate it into our local media, and at the heart of our journalistic endeavours, it would be an innovative and very healthy goal for a small but growing and evolving nation like ours. The East has thrived on the spiritual search for many centuries, yet it is also lacking in its journalism, for journalism is a product of the West, and there is an unconscious movement towards imitating the West in such worldly matters.
>
> But to a great extent the West does not believe in spirituality, and it is suffering great anguish and great anxiety for it. The suicide rate is four times more than in the East. In the East, people commit suicide because of hunger

[65] *Competition Success Review*, August 2010, p. 40.

and starvation — you have to be compassionate towards them. But in the West people commit suicide because they have everything, and they feel life is meaningless. They have all that money can purchase, but they cannot purchase silence, they cannot purchase love, they cannot purchase meditation. Spirituality is the very meaning of life, the very essence of life without a spirit, a man is only a corpse. And without spirituality, anything — sports, education, economics, science, politics, journalism — they are only corpses, they stink.

Therefore the spiritual dimension should be introduced to journalism. And *yoga* and spirituality does not mean any kind of religious fanaticism. Spirituality does not mean that you have to preach Christianity, Hinduism, Islam or Jainism. Spirituality simply means spreading the basic fundamentals of all religions, which are all the same. Can love be Christian or Hindu? Can a peaceful mind be Hindu or Buddhist? Does a man of compassion have to be a Christian or a Jew? An authentic spirituality will be without any adjective. It will only teach the essentials of all religions. And journalism should give it the first preference, on your laundry list, it should be the first item and politics should be the last. Why give so much importance to momentary things? *Yoga* and spirituality means giving importance to something that is of permanent value which gives life, light and guidance forever.

Eternal values constitute spirituality. Momentary values constitute politics. There introduce eternal values to journalism. Why relegate them only to the cultural page or magazines? They are part of the very fabric of life. They should be your major part, and politics should be just your fourth or fifth page. Push politics as far back as possible, to the last pages of your newspapers. Politics is not our soul; it is *yoga* and spirituality which is our soul.

The negative side is part of life, yes! Death is also part of life. But that does not mean you have to make your funeral ground in the middle of the market. It is part of life, so

> once in a while you can talk about the funerals, the wars, but do not focus unnecessarily on them for the sake of sensationalism. Death is certain, but life is more important. Talk about life, make life a celebration. Do not create a phobia with the negative. The media cannot survive on positive news only. That would also be wrong. The negative needs to be brought to the light also, but it should not be emphasized. It should be criticized. The positive should be supported and the negative should be condemned. The negative should be used as a stepping-stone but never emphasized; because that creates the idea in people's minds that the negative is what life is all about, and that is a very dangerous cancer of the soul.[66]

Whatever wrong is happening in media and society is due in degeneration of human values. Therefore if remedy remains in destroying the degeneration of human values, it is *yoga* and spirituality which is the core of human values. The solution for everything lies in *yoga* and spirituality.

The sole aim of journalism should be service and therefore journalism, should never be compromised for selfish ends. Journalism, to be useful and serviceable to individual, society and nation, will take its definite place only when it becomes unselfish, truthful and moral, and such moral values can be endorsed in it only when yogic or spiritual dimension is introduced. The force of ethics and morality would make it follow the right path. Thus *yoga* and spiritual journalism has become more relevant than ever before. The spiritually charged media then would be in a position to give solid solution to all the problems of the individual rather than being a problem itself. Then journalism would unearth those truths and stories which would be in a greater interest of the individual and society, and this positive and healthy journalism, would, indeed usher a new era of love, light and vibrant life for the individual, the society and the nation as well. *Yoga* and spiritual journalism

---

66 www.messagefrommasters.com/Osho

can introduce a noble path in the field of journalism.

It is its approach, its human approach, which would give it writing a character. It will understand people's feelings and give expression to these and can be successful to a great extent, in feeling the pulse of the mute millions. It would then never be a party to exploit the base elements in human beings. It would believe in the nobler trails in a reader and would feed his eternal craving, the quest for truth, bliss and peace.

We agree with Osho that a healthy journalism nourishes the whole personality of a man — his body, his mind and his soul — journalism whose sole concern is to create a better humanity, not just to report what is happening. Journalism should not be just news media, it should also be a great literature, and then it is healthy. Even yesterday's newspaper should remain of some worth so that even today it may be read. But if you are only a news medium then naturally, once the day is passed the news is old. Great literature remains significant, as long as humanity remains, and as fresh as ever. Today's journalism should have that quality. It can have space for news and politics, but they should only be secondary to *yoga* as spirituality is part of the very fabric of life.

And then such positive and healthy journalism based on eternal values like *yoga* and spirituality, would, indeed become the people's Bible, Koran, Zend–Avesta and the *Gita* rolled into one.

5

Practice of Yoga

Practice of Asanas (Yoga Poses)

MAHARSHI Patanjali describes *asana* as the third of the eight limbs of *raja-yoga*. Patanjali describes *asana* as a "steady and comfortable posture",[1] referring specifically to the seated postures used for meditation practices. *Asana* can be defined as a physical *yoga* posture or position that is designed to help master the body and enhance the body's functions. *Yoga* poses are, in essence, *yoga* exercises creating strength and endurance, improving circulation and energy flow, cleansing organs and other systems, and expanding muscles and joints. With all these benefits of the *yoga* poses, we cannot lose attention to the original purpose of the *yoga* pose or *yoga* exercise. *Yoga* exercises evolved thousands of years ago from the need to create a healthy body in order to move more readily to the state of oneness and realization. When the body is cluttered with stress, tension and disease, it clouds the mind and the ability to connect with the inner self. The physical freedom attained from the *yoga* exercises increases one's ability to sit in silence and joyful observation.

Swami Shivanandaji gives some important instructions for *yoga* aspirants. They are as follows[2]:

1. *Asanas* should be practised in a well-ventilated, clean room

---

[1] *Yogasutra* 2.46.

[2] http://elmisattva-nonduality.blogspot.in/2016/02/instructions-on-asanas-by-swami.html

where there is free movement of fresh air. The floor must be even. *Asanas* can be practised on the sandy bed of rivers, open airy places and by the seaside also. If you practise them in a room, see that the room is not congested so as to allow free movement of hands, legs and of the body.

2. *Asanas* should be done on empty stomach in the morning or at least three hours after food. Morning time is the best for doing *asanas*.
3. It is always better to start *japa* and meditation in the early morning at 4 a.m., as soon as you get up from bed. At this time the mind is quite calm and refreshed. You can catch the meditative mood quite easily. Meditation is more important. In the early morning, as soon as you get up from bed, the mind is like a clean slate, free from worldly thoughts. The mind will enter into the meditative mood without effort or struggle.
4. The vast majority of persons waste their precious time in the early morning in answering the calls of nature for half an hour and washing their teeth for another half an hour. The sun rises before they sit for meditation. This is bad. Aspirants should try to defecate within five minutes and cleanse their teeth within five minutes. If one experiences constipation he should do vigorous practice of *salabha*, *bhujanga* and *dhanur asanas* for five minutes as soon as he gets up from bed. If you have the habit of answering the calls of nature late in the day, you can do so after finishing *asanas* and *pranayama*, *japa* and meditation.
5. Get up at 4 a.m. Answer the calls of nature. Wash your face. Be ready for *yoga* practice.
6. Spread a blanket on the floor and practise the *asanas* over the blanket. Use a pillow or fourfolded blanket for practising *shirshasana* and its varieties.
7. During practice it is better to wear loose, light and

comfortable clothing.

8. Do not wear spectacles when you do *asanas*. They may be broken and may injure your eyes.
9. Those who practise *shirshasana*, etc. for a long time should take light tiffin or a cup of milk after finishing the *asana*.
10. If you can devote half an hour or more to *shirshasana* alone, you can cut short the time for other *asanas*.
11. For *asana* practitioners it is better to take natural and healthy diet in moderate quantity.

    mitaharam vina yastu yogarambham tu karayet ।
    nanarogo bhavettasya kinchid yogo na sidhyati ॥
    — *Gheranda Samhita* v.16

    Without observing moderation in diet, if one takes to the yogic practices, he cannot obtain any benefit but gets various diseases.

12. The practice of *asanas* should be ended with *shavasana*. Counterpose must be done. Such as if you have done any forward bending *asana* you should do the counterpose, i.e. any forward bending *asanas*.
13. Be regular in the practice. Those who practise *yoga* occasionally will not derive any benefit.

SURYA-NAMASKARA (SUN SALUTATION)

Sun salutation is considered a complete body workout. *Surya-namaskara* means to bow down to the sun in the morning. The sun is the life source of this planet. In everything that you eat, drink and breathe, there is an element of the sun. Only if you learn how to better "digest" the sun, internalize it, and make it a part of your system, then only you benefit from this process.

Without the sun, there will be no life on earth. *Surya-namaskara* is a very ancient technique of paying respect or expressing gratitude to the sun that is the source of all forms of life on the planet. Symbolically, the sun becomes our source of energy as well.

Surya-namaskara

About the history of this technique, it has been said by the ancient *rishi*s of India that the different parts of the body are governed by different *devas* (divine impulses or divine light).[3] Regular practice of sun salutation offers a lot of interesting benefits for every part of the body. These powerful *yoga* poses have a great impact on the heart, liver, intestine, stomach, chest, throat and legs — the whole body from top to bottom. It purifies the blood and improves blood circulation throughout the body, and ensures proper functioning of the stomach, digestive system and nerve centres. Practising sun salutation daily helps balance the three constitutions — *vata, pitta* and *kapha* — with which the body is made up of.[4]

Step 1: Pranamasana (Prayer Pose)

- Remain standing upright with the feet together.
- Slowly bend the elbows and place the palms together in front of the chest in *pranama/namaskara-mudra.*

---

[3] http://food.ndtv.com/health/the-ultimate-full-body-workout-surya-namaskar-769780

[4] http://www.artofliving.org/in-en/yoga/yoga-poses/surya-namaskar-sun-salutation12-poses-leaner-you

- As you breathe in, lift both your arms up from the sides and as you exhale, bring your palms together in front of the chest in a prayer position.
- Relax the whole body.

Step 2: Hastauttanasana (*Raised Arms Pose*)

- Raise and stretch both arms above the head.
- Keep the arms separated, shoulder width apart.
- Bend the head, arms and upper trunk backward.
- Inhale while raising the arms.

Step 3: Padahastasana/Hastapadasana (*Foot to Hand Pose*)

- Breathing out, bend forward from the waist, keeping the spine erect.
- As you exhale completely, bring the hands down to the floor, beside the feet.
- Now make a gentle effort to straighten the knees.
- It's a good idea to keep the hands fixed in this position and not move them until you finish the sequence.

Step 4: Ashvasanchalanasana (*Equestrian Pose*)

- Breathing in, push your right leg back, as much as possible.
- Bring the right knee to the floor and look up.
- Ensure that the left foot is exactly in between the palms.

Step 5: Parvatasana (*Mountain Pose*)

- Take the left foot back beside the right foot.
- Exhale while taking the left leg back.
- Simultaneously, raise the buttocks and lower the head between the arms, so that the back and legs form two sides of a triangle.
- The legs and arms should be straight in the final position.

- Try to keep the heels on the floor in the final pose and bring the head towards the knees.

Step 6: Ashtanga Namaskarasana (Eight Limbs Salutation Pose)

- Lower the knees, chest and chin to the floor.
- In the final position only the toes, knees, chest, hands and chin touch the floor.
- The knees, chest and chin should touch the floor simultaneously.
- The buttocks, hips and abdomen should be raised.
- The breath is held outside in this pose. There is no respiration.

Step 7: Bhujangasana (Cobra Pose)

- Slide forward and raise the chest up into the cobra posture.
- You may keep your elbows bent in this pose, the shoulders away from the ears. Look up.
- As you inhale, make a gentle effort to push the chest forward; as you exhale, make a gentle effort to push the navel down.
- Tuck the toes under. Ensure you're stretching just as much as you can; do not force your body.

Step 8: Parvatasana (Mountain Pose)

- This step is a repeat of step 5.

Step 9: Ashvasanchalanasana (Equestrian Pose)

- This step is a repeat of step 4.

Step 10: Padahastasana/Hastapadasana (Foot to Hand Pose)

- This step is a repeat of step 3.

Step 11: Hastauttanasana (Raised Arms Pose)

- This step is a repeat of step 2.

Step 12: Pranamasana (Prayer Pose)

- This is the final and is the same as step 1.

This is one round of *surya-namaskara*. You can repeat 4 to 5 rounds comfortably.

Prajna-Yoga[5]

The word *yogasana* (*asana* in brief) refers to a posture in which one feels relaxed while keeping the body active internally. The *rishis* (Vedic sages) had keenly observed the sitting and standing postures of different animals, which, in spite of limited faculties, have wonderful physical capabilities that man is deprived of. They had studied the effects of different postures in the laboratory of their own body and developed specific *asanas* which had rejuvenating effects on the entire body–mind–soul system.

We highlight the main *asanas* of *prajna-yoga*. *Prajna-yoga*, developed by Yugrishi Shriram Sharma Acharya consists of sixteen poses. It is a complete package of *asanas* which has rejuvenating effects on the body, mind and spirit. *Prajna-yoga* can be practised easily by the persons of any age group.

GENERAL GUIDELINES

The beginners should first try to master each of the listed *asanas* one by one separately. Then attempt completing some of them in the desired sequence. Having mastered over the subsequences, one may try the complete sequence of the sixteen *asanas* as described in the following section. Initially it may take extra time but with gradual practice one will be tuned up and complete round of these *asanas* will be over only in about ten minutes. Stand erect. Half-close the eyes and meditating on the brilliance of Lord Savita (power source of rising sun) for a moment chant *om*. Having the faith and inner feeling that the spiritual power of Savita is rejuvenating the body, mind and soul, follow — with each syllable of Gayatri Mantra — the sequence of exercises given underneath. All chantings should be made with deep mental engrossment and steady and deep breathing (inhalation or exhalation, as indicated).

---

[5] http://www.awgp.org/social_initiative/yoga_holistic health/pragya_yog

1. *Tadasana*

Stand on the toes. Chant *bhuh* (*bhooh*) and raise both the hands upward while inhaling gradually and deeply. Look upwards to the sky. (All the four actions should take place simultaneously.) Hold your breath inside. This exercise helps adequate blood supply in the heart, stretching the spine backwards and thus giving it the much-needed rest. This practice instantly removes lethargy. It is also beneficial in the case of weakness of the heart and blood disorders.

2. *Padahastasana*

Chanting *bhuvah*, bring both the hands downward from the posture of *tadasana* and exhale at the same slow and consistent pace and bow the head down to touch the knees, also attempt making the palms touch the floor. Hold your breath out for several seconds and come back to the normal standing posture. Practice of this *asana* removes gastric trouble and induces vital strength in the *ida*, *pingala* and *sushumna nadis*. It also helps reducing tummy fat and increasing the flexibility of the spinal cord.

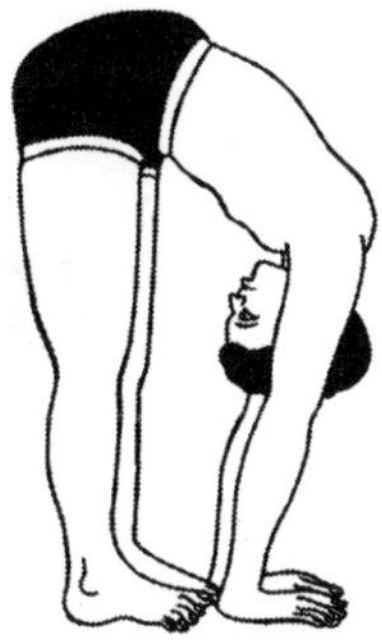

3. *Vajrasana*

With the chant of *svah*, place the toes completely on the floor and set the haunches on the feet. Both the legs should be in closed contact. Keep the backbone erect and place the palms on the knees. Breathe normally during this posture. The back, neck and head should remain straight. Practising this *asana* for few minutes every day is helpful in maintaining good digestion and curing gastric trouble and constipation. It strengthens the muscles around stomach and protects from many stomach problems. Blood supply to the stomach and uterus is finetuned by this practice.

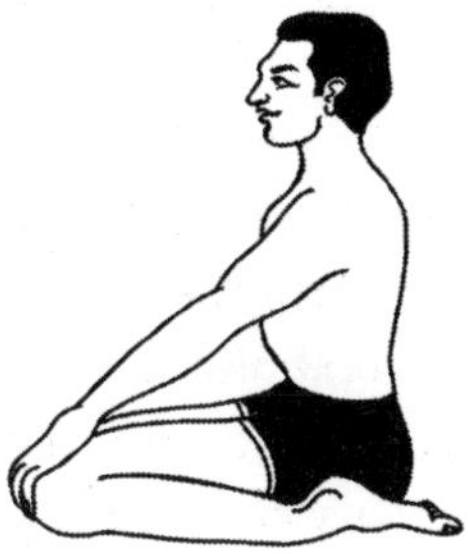

4. *Ushtrasana*

Now get up slightly from the *vajrasana* with a chant of *tat*. Stand on your knees with the toes touching the floor and the heels facing backwards. Almost simultaneously, bend backwards to place the

palms on the heels from the backside. Inhale deeply while looking upwards. This will inflate your chest. Hold the breath in for few seconds. This *asana* stretches the abdomen, stomach, chest, and hands in a balanced way. Practice of this *asana* helps healing the problems of backache and bending of waist/lumber bones, etc. It makes the heart strong and augments the natural elasticity of the spinal column. This also provides exercise to muscles of the genital organs. It is a prerequisite for higher level *yoga* practices of activating the *ida, pingala* and *sushumna.*

5. *Yogamudrasana*

(Remember, the breath was hold inside during the *ushtrasana.*) With the chanting of *savitur*, exhale slowly and sit on your legs as in *vajrasana* at the same time, clench together both the palms at the back and stretch upwardly and place the head on the floor so that the chest and the stomach touch the thighs. Hold the breath out for few seconds. This posture further helps curing severe gastric troubles, setting the metabolic activities right and increasing the appetite. It is recommended in advanced *yoga* practices of awakening the extrasensory energy nucleus called *manipura chakra* beneath the naval.

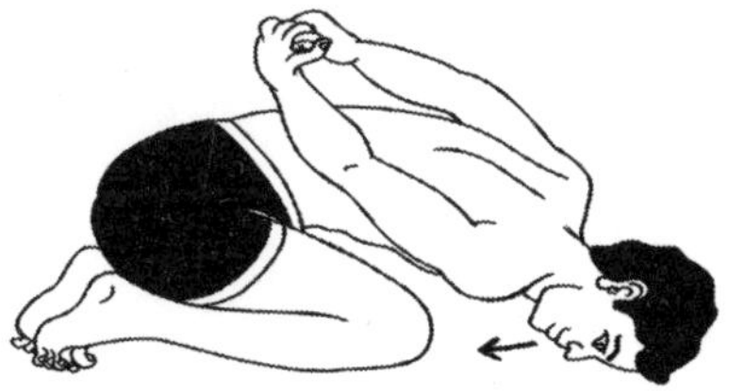

6. *Ardhatadasana*

Chanting *varenyam*, inhale deeply. Being seated in the posture of *vajrasana*, raise both the arms and eyes upwards. Hold the breath inside and raise the arms upward. Focus your eyes on the hands. This *asana* gives a natural and mild traction to the neck and allays the problems, if any, like cervical spondylitis. Likewise *tadasana*, it increases blood supply to the heart and cures weakness of the heart and blood-flow related disorders.

7. *Shashankasana*

Chanting *bhargo*, exhale at the same pace as inhalation in the preceding *asana*. Simultaneously, sit in the posture of *vajrasana* and keep both the arms stretched outwardly in front of the chest. Place the palms on the floor, bend from the waist to make the stomach touch the thighs and the head touch the floor. The arms

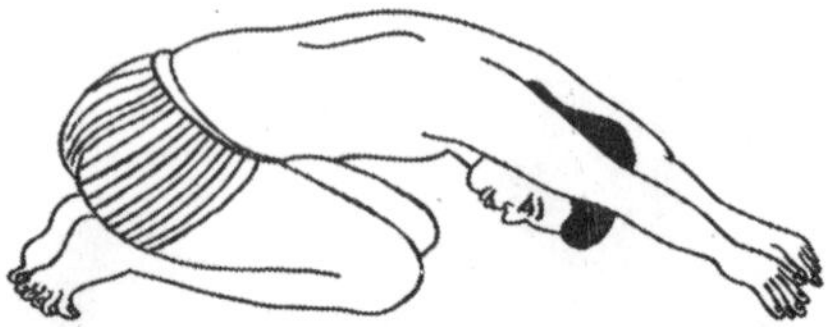

should remain straight with palms touching the floor. Hold the breath outside for few seconds. This *asana* eliminates the problem of constipation and soothingly stretches the muscles within and between the anus and buttock regions. It relaxes the sciatic nerve and also helps in regularizing the secretions from the adrenal gland.

8. *Bhujangasana*

Chanting *devasya* inhale deeply and pull your waist upwards. Toes and palm should remain at the same place where these were in the previous posture but now the arms should stand straighten. The knees and thighs should touch the floor. Draw your chest and head upwards and raise the head like a cobra's hood. Hold the breath inside and bend the head backwards slightly to stare the sky. This exercise is also recommended as a remedy against cervical spondylitis and several other problems of the spine or back. Apart from providing soothing exercise to the lungs, heart and the backbone, it is especially beneficial for healthy functioning of the liver and kidneys.

9. *Tiryak Bhujangasana* (*Left*)

In the posture of *bhujangasana*, exhale slowly. Now inhale and with the chant of *dhimahi* (*dheemahi*) turn the neck towards the left and try looking at the heel of right foot. Then hold the breath for few seconds. With exhalation bring the head in the front.

10. *Tiryak Bhujangasana* (*Right*)

Chant *dhiyo*, inhale and turn the neck towards the right to see the heel of the left foot. Hold the breath for few seconds and bring the head again in the front with exhalation. Practice of the *tiryak bhujangasana* enhances flexibility of the waist and augments the benefits of *bhujangasana*.

11. *Shashankasana*

Chanting *yonah* return to the step 7.

12. *Ardhatadasana*

Chanting *prachodayat* (*prachodayaat*) repeat step 6.

13. *Utkatasana*

After *ardhatadasana* in step 12, exhale slowly. Now chant *bhuh* and with normal breathing sit on the toes. The heels should not touch the floor. Let the calves touch the thighs and knees touch the buttocks. Place both the palms on the knees. Bend the arms

on elbows and keep the hands in front of the chest with palms placed on each other in the posture of *namaskara*. Back, neck and head should be erect. Breathing should be deep and continued at a consistent pace. This *asana* gives strength to the calves and improves balance of the body.

14. *Padahastasana*

Chanting *bhuvah* repeat step 2.

15. *Tadasana*

Chanting *svah* repeat step 1.

16. *Coming Back to Original Position*

With a deep chant of *om*, inhale slowly and deeply, and stand straight with stretched chest. Place the arms upwards and bend the elbows above the shoulders in a posture as though you are holding a heavy rock on the hands. Hold the breath for few seconds with a feeling that your arms, shoulders, chest and whole body are empowered by new vital force. Now close the fists. Exhale slowly, bring the arms on the sides and stand straight in the posture of attention. Breathe normal in a relaxed mood.

These sixteen steps complete one round of the *prajna-yoga asanas*. With gradual progress, one may complete 3 to 5 rounds every day. The breathing patterns and chanting of Gayatri Mantra also get perfected with sincerity in daily practice. To a great extent these also offer the benefits of *pranayamas*. However, if one has time and will or is advised by the *yoga* teacher to do so, the practice of *pranayamas* recommended in the following chapter would render great benefits.

If one continues to practise the above *asanas* aptly and is also sincere in doing *pranayamas* and Gayatri meditation every day at suitable timings (preferably early morning), he would get the physical, mental and spiritual benefits of *ashtanga-yoga*.[6]

---

[6] http://www.awgp.org/social_initiative/yoga_holistic_health/pragya_yog

Practice of Meditative Postures

SUKHASANA (EASY SITTING POSE)

Sukhasana is one of the simplest pose for meditation suited for all beginners. *Sukhasana* comes from the Sanskrit work *sukham* which can mean "comfort" , "easy", "joyful", "pleasure", etc. *Sukhasana* can be done by all age groups.

In many Asian countries, including India, *sukhasana* is part of the daily routine. Traditionally people would take their meals sitting on the floor in *sukhasana*. Hence for them, *sukhasana* is simple. In Western traditions, people usually sit on a chair during meals. Hence many Westerners find it difficult to sit on the floor in the cross-legged position. But *sukhasana* is the simplest of the sitting postures in *yoga*. It is easy to perform and can be done even by elderly people. But, those with serious knee or hip injuries should avoid this posture.

Practice

- Sit down normally on the floor. (If you are not used to sitting on the floor or you are uncomfortable, then keep one thick folded blanket on the floor for firm and flat base for sitting.) Stretch out your legs ahead in front.
- Now cross your legs and broaden your knees, in order that you can slip your both foot under the opposite knee.
- After that you have to bend your knees, folding your legs.
- Keep your feet loose, in order that the external edges lay on the

floor and the inner curves are settled beneath the inverse leg.

- Your thighs and crossed legs ought to frame a little triangle. Keep some space between your feet and pelvis.
- Now sit with your buttock in a neutral position. (For this, you have to press your hands opposing the ground and lift your sitting bones a bit.) Attempt to hold for a breath or two and after that gradually bring down yourself back on to the floor.
- Balance your tail bone and pubic bone in a manner that they are equidistant from the floor.
- Keep your hands on your knees with palm facing down and expand your tailbone against the floor. (You can keep your hands in *jnana-mudra*.)

Advantages

- It stretches and lengthens your spine.
- Broadens your collarbones and chest.
- It calms your mind.
- Enhances your condition of peacefulness and serenity.
- Kicks out anxiety, stress and mental tiredness.
- It helps in improving body posture.
- It helps in reducing fatigue.
- It strengthens your back.
- It stretches your ankles and knees.
- It gives gentle massage to your knees, calf muscles and thighs.

Precaution

As the name proposes, the *sukhasana yoga* stance is known as a simple stance and comfortable *asana*. Therefore it doesn't have excessively numerous contraindications. Individuals who are experiencing backache or back agony shouldn't stay in this position for over 5 minutes. People who have experienced the knee injury are advised not to sit in this position for a long time. Avoid this in case of joint or knee-related problems.

SVASTIKASANA

Svastika is an auspicious tantric symbol. It is a symbol of fertility and creativity. As this *asana* resembles *svastika*, it is called as *svastikasana*. In *Hatha-Yoga Pradipika*, *svastikasana* is described as: *janurvarantare samyakritva padatale utherujukayaha samasinaha svastikam tatprachakshate.* (Having firmly inserted both foots between the thighs and knees, he should sit erect on a level place.) This is *svastikasana.*

Practice

- Stretch the legs to the front.
- Put the right foot in between left thigh and knee.
- In this position the right foot is entirely immersed in between left thigh and left knee.
- Likewise put the left foot in between right thigh and knee from below the knee.
- Neck and back should be straight. Put the palms on knees, upwards, join thumb and index finger, and this is called *yoga-mudra.*
- The sight should be focused on the tip of the nose.

Advantages

- This is one of the simplest and comfortable meditative posture.
- This *asana* is very comfortable for long hours of meditation.
- It is most suitable for *pranayama*, meditation, learning and spiritual activities.

- This *asana* reduces the high blood pressure.
- Ailments of knees are cured from the practice of this *asana*.
- As the backbone is kept straight in this *asana*, pressure on spinal cord is relieved thereby strengthening the backbone.
- Flow of energy in *nadis* (energy channels in the subtle body) will increase.
- Cleansing of *nadis* is one of the main benefits of this *asana*.
- A pleasant feeling in the body arises and calmness pervades the body and mind.
- Auspicious vibrations and feelings will enter the mind as the name of the *asana* is *svastika* which means auspicious.
- *Kundalini* power is awakened by the regular practice of *svastikasana*.
- This *asana* tones the muscles of abdominal area and sciatic nerve.
- Normal temperature in the body is maintained by the regular practice of *svastikasana*.

SIDDHASANA

Siddhasana (accomplished pose) is an *asana* used for meditation and other yogic practices. In Sanskrit *siddha* means "accomplished" or an "adept" and *asana* means a "pose". *Siddhasana* is mentioned in *Hatha-Yoga Pradipika* as one of the four most powerful sitting poses suited for meditation.

For practitioners of meditation, the importance of *siddhasana* is only second to *padmasana* (lotus pose). In fact, some claim *siddhasana* to be the best of all *asanas* for meditation. In *Hatha-Yoga Pradipika*, it is said that a *yoga* practitioner should always practise *siddhasana*, among the 84 *asanas*. The text says that practice of *siddhasana* purifies all the 72,000 *nadis* (energy channels) in the body, through which the *prana* flows. It also says that by contemplating on one's Self, eating moderately and practising *siddhasana* for twelve years, one can attain success in *yoga*. This *asana* can be practised by anyone, except those suffering from sciatica or sacrum infections.

Practice

- Sit on the floor with legs close to each other.
- Take the left foot and place it at the perineum. The perineum is the soft tissue between the anus and the testis. For females, it is done differently. Females should place the left foot in the *labia majora* of the vagina.
- Now take the right foot and place it over the left foot.
- To make the posture steadier, slide the right foot toes into the space between the left calf muscles. This may require some adjustment to the position. It is like creating a lock, so that the lower body is stable for long durations of meditation.
- The knees should touch the floor.
- Now, make your spine straight.
- The chin can press against the chest.
- Gaze at the space between the eyebrows. And become aware of your breathing process. The breathing can be natural and deep. One may also practise *ujjayi* breathing according to one's meditation technique.
- The hands can be kept on the knees. One may assume the *chin-mudra* or the *jnana-mudra* with the fingers, if one wishes.
- Maintain this position for as long as you are comfortable.

Advantages

- *Siddhasana* is one of the main poses used for meditation. One can maintain this position for a long duration. Those who have difficulty in practising *padmasana* can easily practise *siddhasana* for extended periods. This *asana* holds the spinal column straight and steady.

- In *siddhasana*, the heel is kept pressed against the *muladhara chakra*. This ensures that the energy currents flow upwards towards the spine.
- The position of the heels also stimulates the lower two *chakras*: *muladhara* and *svadhishthana*. The sexual energy is channelized upwards and converted into subtle energy called *ojas*.
- It also gives the practitioner control over his sex urge and the sexual functions.
- In *Hatha-Yoga Pradipika*, it is said that *siddhasana* stabilizes the nervous system by calming down the pranic energy.

PADMASANA

Padmasana (lotus pose) is an important meditative *asana* and is mentioned in most yogic texts. In Sanskrit, *padma* means lotus and *asana* means pose. *Padmasana* is mentioned in the yogic text *Hatha-Yoga Pradipika* as one of the main *asana*s for meditation that can destroy all diseases. If you see the drawings and sculptors of ancient *yogi*s, you will notice that they are seated in *padmasana*. Ancient statues of Shiva, the Buddha and Mahavira are all depicted as sitting in *padmasana*. The hand *mudra*s may vary, but the legs are always shown seated in the lotus pose.

Padmasana is considered as one of the best poses for meditation. In *padmasana*, the legs are locked together and the lower body is absolutely stable. Also, the back and spine will be straight. This is perfect for longer periods of meditation as the body can be held motionless, with least distractions.

Padmasana is not easy for beginners. In the Eastern traditions, people are used to sitting on the floor in the simple cross-legged position, especially for meals. But in the Western tradition, most people use chairs for sitting during meals. In such cases, a little

practice will be required to bring flexibility into the legs. One can do any exercise that stretches the lower legs, thigh and waist muscles to get this flexibility. Also the joints (ankles, knee and waist) should be made supple by doing *pavanamuktasana* series of exercises. Those suffering from sciatica and sacrum infection, weak knee joints, etc. should avoid this *asana*.

Practice

- Sit on the floor comfortably.
- Slowly and carefully bend one leg and place the foot on top of the opposite thigh.
- Now bend the other leg and place the foot on the top of the opposite thigh.
- Both knees should ideally touch the ground in the final position.
- The head and spine should be held upright.
- Place the hands on the knees in *chin-mudra* or *jnana-mudra*.
- You may close your eyes. Breathe slowly and deeply. Let the awareness be on the breathing process. Experience the perfect balance and alignment of the entire body.
- Maintain this position for as long as comfortable. Those

who wish to use this pose for meditation should sit for at least 20 minutes. Slowly increase it so that your duration of meditation too can increase. At some point the legs may start to pain. Once you have crossed your threshold of pain, slowly release the legs and massage them gently, till the ache is gone. Over a period of time, you will be able to sit for long duration in this *asana*. Those who are young will master this *asana* quickly. After an age of 30-35 years, the body is less supple. Of course, with practice anyone, even those above 60 years, can master this *asana*. It is said that if one can sit in an *asana* for three and half hours, one is said to have attained *siddhi* in that *asana*. One need not go to such extremes; even 30 minutes to an hour is good enough for most practitioners.

- One of the main points to be noted in meditative *asanas* is that the body should be absolutely still and relaxed. There should be no pains or stress, otherwise instead of meditating, attention will be drawn to the body and its discomforts. One may use a soft support (soft pillow, cushion, etc.) under the buttocks to feel comfort.
- *Padmasana* can also be done with the left leg over the right leg. In this case, first the right leg is placed on the left thigh. Then the left leg is place over the right thigh. But traditionally, it is practised the other way (with right leg over left leg). If you notice statues of Lord Buddha which are excavated from ancient temples, which are over 2,000 years old, you will see that the right leg is placed over the left leg.
- In the yogic text *Hatha-Yoga Pradipika*, it is mentioned that one can gaze at the tip of the nose and keep the tongue touching the roof of the palette (behind the teeth) during meditation in *padmasana*. This is supposed to help the *prana* (*apana vayu*) raise up the spine.

Position of Hands in Padmasana

Padmasana can also be done with hands resting on the knees. In this case, the elbows are slightly bent and the hands rest on the knees, with palms facing upwards. *Chin-mudra* or *jnana-mudra* can also be performed with the fingers.

Advantages

- *Padmasana* is considered as one of the best *asanas* for meditation. The body can be held steady and straight for long durations.
- When there is hardly any distraction from the body, the mind can be made calm. Awareness of the breathing process also helps to steady the mind. The body and mind are intricately connected. A steady body can bring steadiness in the mind.
- The spine is kept straight and this helps to channel the energy from the lower spiritual centres (*chakras*) upwards towards *sahasrara chakra*. The erect spine aids the free flow of *prana* along the spinal cord.
- *Padmasana* can tone the coccygeal and sacral nerves as the blood flow to the legs are restricted and redirected to the abdominal region. It may improve digestion too.
- Sitting in *padmasana* can relieve many metal and emotional problems.
- In *Hatha-Yoga Pradipika* it is said that if a *yogi* can control breathing sitting in *padmasana*, he can become free of all bondages. Hence it is an excellent *asana* for practising advanced *pranayama* techniques.

Some Other Important Asanas

VAJRASANA

Vajrasana is the simple *asana* which can be practised after lunch or dinner also. *Vajrasana* is also known as "diamond pose" which is best for practising breathing exercises and meditation. Regular practice makes you stronger and healthier.

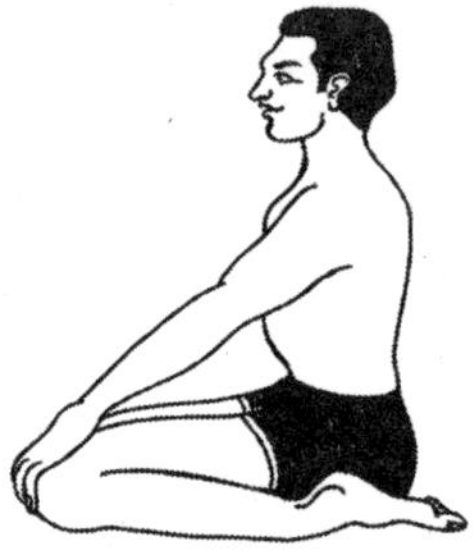

Practice

- Sit on the floor on a mat or directly on the ground.
- Fold your legs and sit in such a manner that heels touch the sides of the hips.
- Place the hands on the knees, palms down.
- The back and head should be straight but not tense.
- Close the eyes, relax the arms and the whole body.
- Breathe normally and fix the attention on the flow of air passing in and out of the nostrils.
- Hold the sitting pose for two minutes (to start with). You will feel a stinging pain in your feet if you are not habitual to sitting this way. You can stretch your legs and rest for a while and start again.
- Sit for a minimum of two minutes. You should increase the minutes over time. It is even possible to sit on *vajrasana* pose for almost half an hour.
- It's considered the best to do *vajrasana* just after having food but you can do it at any time of the day.

Advantages

- This *asana* performed immediately after food aids the rate of digestion.
- Regular practice of *vajrasana* relieves constipation, acidity and induces digestion process.
- It also rids off back pain, stomach disorder and urinary problems.
- It strengthens the sexual organs and increases blood circulation.
- It is a preferred posture for meditation and concentration.

Precautions and Contraindications

- A person suffering from joint pain should avoid this *asana.*
- People who have any spinal column ailments, especially on the lower vertebrae should not attempt this pose. Those with hernia, intestinal ulcers should avoid this *asana.*

Duration

Practise *vajrasana* for 15 to 20 minutes after lunch or dinner. You can increase the period as long as you can.

PASHCHIMOTTANASANA (FORWARD BEND POSE)

Pashchima means your "back" and *uttana* means "stretching". This *asana* covers the stretching of the whole body from head to heels so it is called as *pashchimottanasana.*

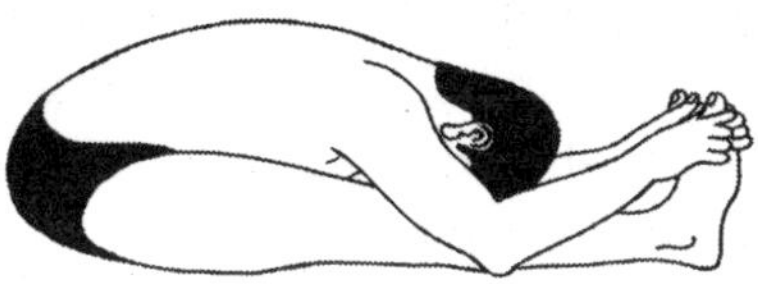

Practice

- Sit down straight with your legs together by stretching in front of you. Keep your head, neck and spine erect.
- Place the palms on your respective knees.

- Now bend your head and trunk slowly forward to catch the toes with the thumb, index and middle fingers without bending knees.
- Take a deep breath and exhale slowly. Try to touch your head both knees as shown in above image.
- Bend the arms and try to touch the elbows on the floor.
- Exhale completely and holding out your breath stay in this posture for a few seconds.
- After a few seconds slowly return to your starting position.
- Breathe normally.
- Repeat this for 3-4 times.

Advantages

- Soothes headache and anxiety and reduces fatigue.
- Calms the brain and helps relieve stress and mild depression.
- Stretches the spine, shoulders, hamstrings.
- Stimulates the liver, kidneys, ovaries and uterus.
- Improves digestion.
- Therapeutic for high blood pressure, infertility, insomnia, and sinusitis.
- Traditional texts say that *pashchimottanasana* increases appetite, reduces obesity and cures diseases.
- Helps relieve the symptoms of menopause and menstrual discomfort.

Precautions

- Pregnant women should not practise *pashchimottanasana.*
- Person suffering from slip disc or sciatica, back injury, diarrhoea, asthma should avoid *pashchimottanasana.*
- Ulcer patients should not practise it.

DHANURASANA (BOW POSE)

Dhanurasana has been named after the shape the body takes while performing it — that of a bow. *Dhanu* means bow; *asana* means posture or pose.

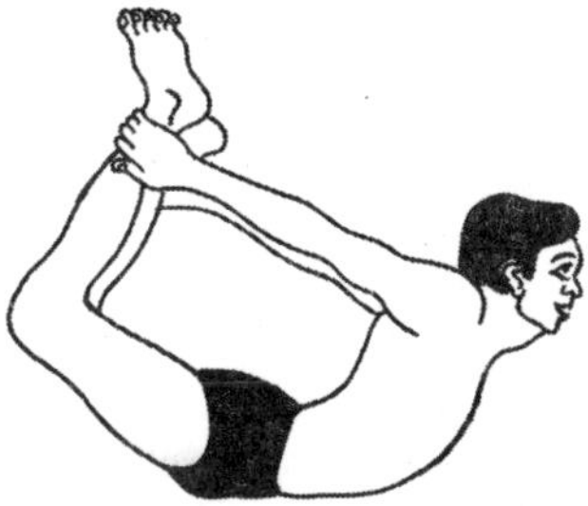

Practice

- Lie on your stomach with your feet hip-width apart and your arms by the side of your body.
- Fold your knees, take your hands backwards and hold your ankles.
- Breathing in, lift your chest off the ground and pull your legs up and back.
- Look straight ahead with a smile on your face.
- Keep the pose stable while paying attention to your breath. Your body is now curved and taut as a bow.
- Continue to take long deep breaths as you relax in this pose. But bend only as far as your body permits you to. Do not overdo the stretch.
- After 15-20 seconds, as you exhale, gently bring your legs and chest to the ground. Release the ankles and relax.

Advantages

- Strengthens the back and abdominal muscles.
- Stimulates the reproductive organs.
- Opens up the chest, neck and shoulders.
- Tones the leg and arm muscles.
- Adds greater flexibility to the back.
- Good stress and fatigue buster.
- Relieves menstrual discomfort and constipation.
- Helps people with renal (kidney) disorders.

Precaution

Do not practise *dhanurasana* if you have:

- High or low blood pressure.
- Hernia.
- Neck injury.
- Pain in the lower back.
- Headache, migraine.
- Recent abdominal surgery.

Ladies should avoid practising this *yoga* pose during pregnancy.

SHAVASANA (CORPSE POSE)

This pose gets its name from the posture of a dead body. It is a position of rest and relaxation, and is usually practised towards the end of a *yoga* session.

Practice

- Lie flat on the back with the arms about 15 cm away from the body, palms facing upwards. Use small pillow below your neck if absolutely required. Close your eyes.
- Keep your legs comfortably apart and let your feet and knees relax completely, toes facing to the sides.
- Place your arms alongside, yet a little spread apart from your body. Leave your palms open, facing upward.
- Taking your attention to different body parts one by one, slowly relax your entire body.
- Begin with bringing your awareness to the right foot, move on to the right knee (as you complete one leg, move your attention on to the other leg), and so on, and slowly move

upwards to your head, relaxing each part of the body.

- Keep breathing slowly, gently, deeply and allow your breath to relax you more and more. The incoming breath energizes the body while the outgoing breath brings relaxation. Drop all sense of hurry or urgency or any need to attend to anything else. Just be with the body and the breath. Surrender the whole body to the floor and let go. Make sure you don't fall asleep!
- After some time, about 10-20 minutes when you feel fully relaxed, keeping your eyes closed, slowly roll onto your right side. Lie in that position for a minute or so. Then, taking the support of your right hand, gently sit up into a seated pose such as *sukhasana* (easy pose).
- Keep your eyes closed and take a few deep breaths in and out as you gradually become aware of your environment and the body. When you feel complete, slowly and gently open your eyes.

Advantages

- This posture brings a deep, meditative state of rest, which may help in the repair of tissues and cells, and in releasing stress. It also gives time for the *yoga* workout to sink in at a deeper level.
- This posture leaves you in a state of rejuvenation. It is the perfect way to end a *yoga* session, particularly if it has been a fast-paced one.
- It helps reduce blood pressure, anxiety and insomnia.
- This is an excellent way to ground the body and reduce the *vata dosha* (imbalance of the air element) in the body.

Precaution

None (unless your doctor has advised you, for some medical reason, to avoid lying on your back).

Pranayama

Pranayama is a Sanskrit word which consists of *prana* and *ayama*. *Prana* means life force or vital energy and *ayama* means extension. *Pranayama* may be defined as expansion and control of *prana*. *Pranayama* is not a simple breathing exercise rather it is a scientific breathing process. In a simple way, we can say that *pranayama* is a combination of systematic exhalation and inhalation.

Pranayama is said to be the union of *prana* and *apana*. *Pranayama*, in the language of *yoga*, means the process by which we understand the secret of *prana* and control it. He, who has grasped this *prana*, has grasped the very core of cosmic life and activity. He who has conquered and controlled this very essence, has not only subjected his own body and mind, but every other body, mind and power in this universe. Thus, *pranayama* (control of *prana*) is that means by which the *yogi* tries to realize in his little body the whole of cosmic life and tries to attain perfection by getting all the powers in the universe. His various exercises and training are for this end. A comprehensive knowledge of *prana* and its function is absolutely necessary for *pranayama*.

PRANIC BODY

According to yogic physiology, the human body is comprised of five bodies or sheaths, which account for the different aspects or dimensions of human existence. They are as follows:

1. *Annamaya kosha* (food or material body)
2. *Manomaya kosha* (mental body)
3. *Pranamaya kosha* (vital energy body)
4. *Vijnanamaya kosha* (psychic or higher mental body)
5. *Anandamaya kosha* (transcendental or bliss body).

Although these five sheaths function together to form an integral whole, the practices of *pranayama* work mainly with *pranamaya kosha*. The *pranamaya kosha* is made up of five major *pranas* which are collectively known as the *pancha* (five) *pranas*:

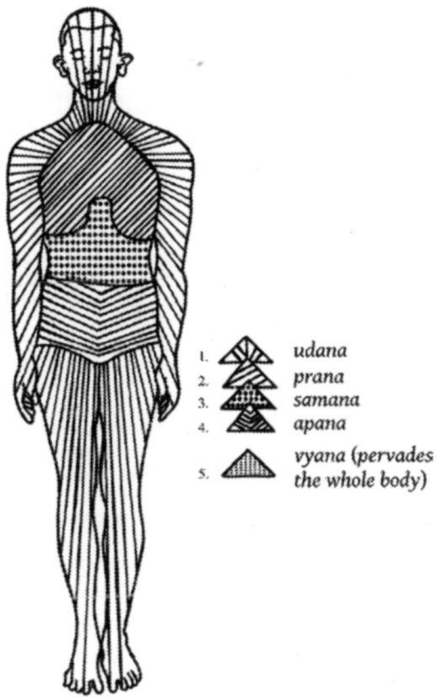

prana, apana, samana, udana and *vyana.*[7]

1. *Prana* is located in the region between the larynx and the top of the diaphragm. It is traditionally associated with the respiratory organs, the organs of speech, the gullet, etc. It is the force by which the breath is drawn in. *Prana* is also said to work in the mouth and nose, and it is responsible for converting water into sweat and urine, as well as controlling glandular secretions.
2. *Apana* is located below the navel region and provides the energy for the large intestines, kidneys and the functioning of the anus and reproductive organs. It is also said to circulate between the navel and soles of the feet.
3. *Samana* is located in the region between the heart and the navel. It activates and controls the digestive system, the liver, pancreas and the stomach. It is responsible for the digestion as well as the assimilation of nutrients.

---

[7] Saraswati, 2002, *Asana, Pranayama, Mudra, Bandha*, p. 365.

4. *Udana* controls the parts of the body above the larynx. The eyes, nose, ears and sensory receptors in all parts of the body are activated by this *prana*. It is also responsible for maintaining muscular strength.
5. *Vyana* is the force which pervades the whole body. It regulates and controls the overall movements of the body and co-ordinates the other vital energies.

There is another subdivision of the pranic force called the *upa-pranas*. They are responsible for minor transformations of energy, as for example, when we sneeze, yawn, belch, hiccup or blink our eyes. These minor (*upa*) *pranas* are called *naga*, *kurma*, *krikara*, *devadatta* and *dhananjaya*. Traditionally these *pranas* are controlled by *vayus* (currents or winds), which are generated by the process of breathing and, allied with that, certain practices of concentration. The *vayus* are like energy corridors along which each particular division of the pranic force flows, internally and also externally.

PRANA

Prana is the sum total of all energy that is manifest in the universe. It is the sum total of all the forces of nature. Heat, light, electricity, magnetism are all the manifestations of *prana*. All forces, all powers and *prana* spring from the fountain or common source – *atman*. *Prana* is the very essence of cosmic life, that subtle principle which evolves the whole universe into its present form and which is pushing it towards its ultimate goal. *Prana* may be defined as the finest vital force in everything which becomes visible on the physical plane as motion and action and on the mental plane as thought. That which travels in the nerves of the physical body is gross *prana*. That which moves in astral tubes (*yoga nadis*) of the astral body is subtle *prana* (psychic *prana*). Breath is an external effect or manifestation of gross *prana*. There is intimate connection between the gross *prana* and subtle *prana*.

The function of mind belongs to *prana*; from *prana* (life) proceeds all (*Chhandogya Upanishad* V.14-15). If *prana* departs from the body, all functions of organs cease immediately.

Though *prana* is one, it assumes five forms, viz. *prana, apana, samana, udana* and *vyana* according to the different functions it performs as we have seen already. The principal *prana* is called *mukhya prana*. The function of *mukhya prana* is respiration; *apana* does excretion; *udana* does deglutition; *vyana* performs circulation of blood and *samana* does digestion.

YOGA NADIS

Nadis are the astral tubes made up of astral matter that carry the subtle *prana*. It is through these *nadis* that the vital force of pranic current moves. Since these are made up of subtle matter, these cannot be seen by the naked eyes. These *yoga nadis* are not ordinary nerves, arteries and veins that are known to Vaidya Shastra. The body is filled with innumerable number of *nadis* that cannot be counted. *Nadis* play a vital part in this *yoga*. These subtle tubes (*yoga nadis*) have influence in the physical body.

CHAKRAS

Wherever there is an interlacing of several nerves, arteries and veins, that centre is called as plexus. Similarly there are plexuses or centres of vital forces in the *sukshma nadis*. These are called as *chakras* or *padmas*. All *nadis* spring from *kanda*. It is in the junction where the *sushumna nadi* is connected with the *muladhara chakra*. Of the innumerable *nadis, ida, pingala* and *sushumna* are the most important. *Ida* and *pingala nadis* are on the two sides of the spinal cord and *sushumna* is within the spinal cord. *Ida* operates through the left nostril and *pingala* through the right nostril. When the breath operates through *sushumna*, the mind becomes steady. This steadiness of mind is termed *unmani avastha*, the highest state in *raja-yoga*. If you sit for meditation when *sushumna* is operating, you will have wonderful meditation. When the *nadis* are full of impurities, the breath cannot pass through the middle *nadi*. So, one

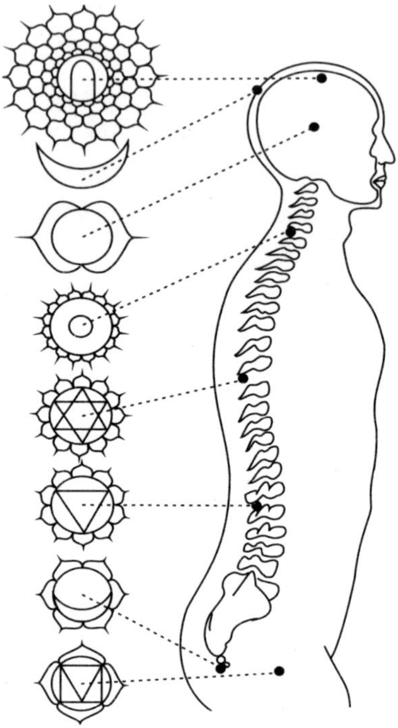

Location of the *chakras*

should practise *pranayama* for the purification of *nadis*.[8]

In the physical body we have two types of energies. One is known as *prana* and the other is known as mind or consciousness. That means, in every organ of the body there should be two channels supplying energy. Modern physiology describes two types of nervous systems — the sympathetic and the parasympathetic, and these two nervous systems are interconnected with each and every organ of the body. In the same way, every organ is supplied with the energy of *prana* and the energy of mind.

In *yoga*, the concept of *prana* is very scientific. When we speak of *prana*, we do not mean the breath, air or oxygen. Precisely and

---

[8] http://sivanandaonline.org/public_html/?cmd=displaysection&section_id=839

scientifically speaking, *prana* means the original life force.

Prana is a Sanskrit word constructed of the syllables *pra* and *an*. *An* means movement and *pra* is a prefix meaning constant. Therefore, *prana* means constant motion. This constant motion commences in the human being as soon as he is conceived in his mother's womb. *Prana* is therefore a type of energy responsible for the body's life, heat and maintenance.

NADIS, CHAKRAS AND THE DISTRIBUTION OF PRANA

According to *yoga*, Tantra and the science of *kundalini*, *prana* is supposed to originate from *pingala nadi*. Within the framework of the spinal cord, there are three channels known as *nadis* in *yoga*. One is called *ida*, another is *pingala* and the third is *sushumna*. *Ida nadi* represents the mental energy, *pingala* represents *prana* or pranic

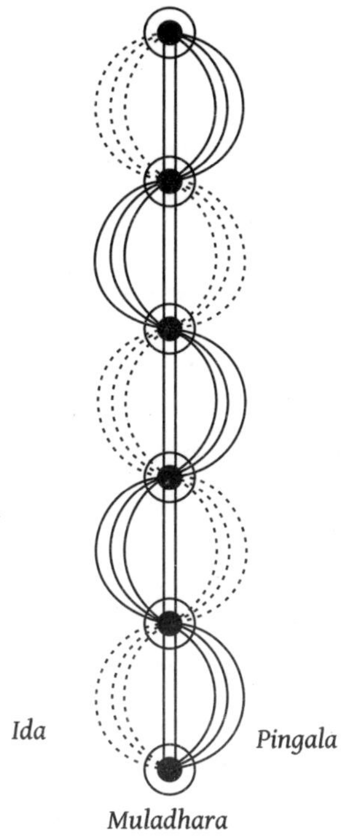

energy and *sushumna* represents spirit or spiritual awareness. These three *nadis* originate in *muladhara chakra*, which is situated at the perineum or cervix. *Pingala nadi* flows to the right from *muladhara* and continues to cross *ida* at each *chakra* all the way up to *ajna*.

It is *chakras* through which *pingala nadi* passes. The first one is *muladhara chakra* from which it originates. The second is *svadhishthana* where the *nadi* crosses to the left. The third is *manipura chakra* where the *nadi* crosses to the right. And the fourth is *anahata* where the *nadi* crosses to the left. The fifth is *vishuddhi* where the *nadi* crosses to the right and the sixth is *ajna* where the *nadi* terminates from the right. Similarly, *ida nadi* also crosses at each *chakra* but in the reverse order. Every sincere *yoga* aspirant should have a clear understanding of the pathway of these three major *nadis*.

Pingala nadi is the distributing channel for *prana* in the body, and from each *chakra* the *prana* is disseminated to every organ of the body. From *svadhishthana* the pranic energy is distributed to the genito-urinary system. *Manipura chakra* supplies *prana* to the digestive system and *anahata* supplies the respiratory and cardiovascular systems. From *vishuddhi*, distribution takes place to the ears, eyes, nose and throat, and *ajna chakra* is the distributor of energy through which man's brain is fed.

THE FUEL OF LIFE

Prana is not merely a philosophical concept; it is in every sense a physical substance. Just as radioactive or electromagnetic waves exist even though we can't see them, in the same way, in this physical body, there are pranic waves and a pranic field. Now, each of us has a certain quantity of *prana* in our physical body and we utilize this in the course of our day-to-day activities throughout life. When our *prana* diminishes, sickness sets in, and when we have plenty of *prana*, every part of the body is in perfect health. If we have an excess of *prana*, it can be transmitted to others for healing or magnetism.

The inner *prana* can be stimulated by the practice of *pranayama* and thereby increased to a greater quantum. The brain requires maximum *prana*, and for the practice of meditation, it needs an increased supply. It is for this reason that we practise *pranayama* before commencing our meditation practice. If we are not able to supply plenty of pranic fuel to the brain, the mind becomes very restless and disturbed.

UNITING WITH THE UNIVERSAL PRANA

Prana is not only the life force, it is also a very powerful healing force in the body that can even eradicate the most difficult physical problems. Moreover, the *prana* within us is a part of the universal *prana*. I am not talking about positive and negative ions now, I am speaking of a metaphysical substance. This is called universal *prana* and our *prana* is a part of that. If one can unite him with the universal *prana*, he can draw the required amount of *prana* as and when needed.

In order to tune oneself to this universal *prana*, he must be able to reach a high state of meditation. When one controls the breath, his mind is also controlled and the awareness becomes one-pointed. That one-pointed awareness is comprehended in the mid-eyebrow centre where the point is seen as a light. The light grows in intensity and becomes bigger and bigger until it completely envelops one's consciousness. Then there is illumination all around the person, and at this point he can connect oneself with the universal *prana*.

It is very difficult for us to attune ourselves to the universal *prana* because our awareness is very limited. Most of us only know about deep breathing, and we think that by breathing deeply fifty to a hundred times, we will get more and more *shakti*. Of course, we do, but we need a finer form of *prana shakti* which can be used for awakening the brain.

Throughout a person's body there is a pranic field which is known as *pranamaya kosha*. One must know how to tune this *pranamaya kosha* with the universal *prana*. *Pranamaya kosha* can be awakened by practising *pranayama* correctly, by fasting or eating properly, and by perfecting meditation on the mid-eyebrow centre. When one sees that great enveloping light, he becomes the medium of the universal *prana*. Thereafter, he can distribute this *prana* to those who have it in short supply.

PRANAYAMA IS NOT A SIMPLE BREATHING EXERCISE

In the *pranayama* practice, four important aspects of breathing are used. They are:

1. *Puraka* (inhalation)
2. *Rechaka* (exhalation)
3. *Antar kumbhaka* (internal breath retention)
4. *Bahir kumbhaka* (external retention).

There is a difference between *pranayama* and breathing process. *Pranayama* is not a simple breathing process; it is much more than inhalation and exhalation. *Pranayama* is a regulated breathing, which comprises *puraka* – slow and prolonged inhalation, *kumbhaka* — retention of breathe, and *rechaka* — slow and prolonged exhalation. While breathing involves inhalation and exhalation, *Pranayama* is always performed in a specific posture, especially sitting in *padmasana* while in case of breathing, it is not so like that. Breathing provides physical benefits while *pranayama* involves physical, mental and spiritual benefits.

FOR THE PRACTICE OF PRANAYAMA

Pranayama should be practised at a place which is free from dust, pollutants, smoke and filthy things. The sitting ground should be flat and smooth. The suitable time for performing *pranayama* is early in the morning on empty stomach. To have the proper benefits, one should practise *pranayama* regularly. *Pranayama* facilitates better blood circulation in the body when it is done after bath. One should ensure that breathing should be through nose and it should be slow and rhythmic. During *pranayama*, eyes should be closed to control the mind and body.

SIGNIFICANCE

- Increases and enhances the quantity and quality of *prana*.
- Makes one energetic, enthusiastic and positive.
- Brings harmony between the body, mind and spirit, making one physically, mentally and spiritually strong. It brings clarity to the mind and good health to the body.

There are some specific *pranayamas* which can be practised with ease and at any time of the day on an empty stomach.

BHASTRIKA PRANAYAMA

Bhastrika pranayama is one of the main forms of *pranayama*. In Sanskrit, *bhastrika* means the "bellows". Just as the blacksmith blows his bellows to create heat and purify iron, *bhastrika* is said to purify the mind and clear pranic blocks. *Bhastrika* is mentioned in the *yoga* texts *Hatha-Yoga Pradipika* and *Gheranda Samhita*.

Bhastrika involves both rapid inhalation as well as exhalation. This helps to increase the circulation of blood in the entire body. During rapid and forced exhalation, the chest is compressed, thereby pushing the blood towards the head. During the inhalation, the reverse takes place. This process increases the blood flow to every part of the body, increasing the vitality of all the organs and tissues. Long-term practice of *bhastrika* purifies the body and awakens the inherent higher powers. *Bhastrika* can be practised both in the morning and evening. During summer, if the temperature is high, the practice should be restricted to mornings only. *Bhastrika*

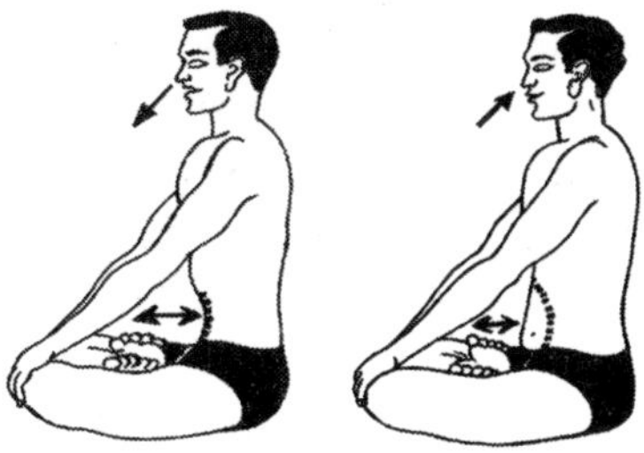

is an advanced practice and should be done on an empty stomach, after evacuation in the morning. Those who take up prolonged practice of *bhastrika*, should take only light meals during morning and night. The lunch can be normal.

Those suffering from heart diseases should not do this *pranayama*. Also avoid it when you have a severe block of the nose. Those with acute asthma and fever should also not attempt *bhastrika*. If you had any recent surgery, please consult your doctor before attempting *bhastrika*. Practice of *bhastrika* can be little intense for some people. It should be learned only under the guidance of a qualified *yoga* instructor. In case of any existing medical conditions, please consult your doctor before taking up the practice.

Duration

There should be inhalation of 2½ seconds and exhalation of 2½ seconds in a rhythmic flow.

Non-stop, one can do *bhastrika pranayama* 12 times in one minute. One should do it for 5 minutes in one sitting. In the beginning one may have to take rest in between. It takes about a week to develop the practice of this *pranayama* for 5 minutes non-stop. Healthy persons and slightly sick persons should practice for 5 minutes daily. Those who are suffering from cancer, lung fibrosis, muscular dystrophy, multiple sclerosis (MS), systemic lupus erythematosus (SLE) and other incurable diseases should do this *pranayama* for 10 minutes. If done in two sittings in incurable diseases like cancer this *pranayama* is best done 120 times. If for some reason one is not able to do *pranayama* in the morning it can also be done 5 hours after midday meals. If persons suffering from incurable diseases practise *pranayama* both in the morning and evening, they will soon benefit more.

Practice

- Sit in any comfortable *asana*. *Padmasana*, *siddhasana* and *vajrasana* are ideal for the practice.

- Inhale and exhale in rapid succession. During this process a hissing sound is produced. Between the rounds, rest for a while, till the breathing comes back to normal.
- Inhaling and exhaling should take the same length of time — 2½ seconds to breathe in and 2½ seconds to breathe out.
- While you breathe in (inhale), assume that we are taking in positive energy and vibrations, and that we are being energized by them. One should think (resolve) in his mind whatever is noble and pure in the universe, such as divine power, energy, sanctity, serenity and bliss, is instilling into his body along with *prana*. He is getting suffused with divine powers. The *pranayama* done with this divine resolution is essentially beneficial.
- During breathe out (exhale), imagine that we are taking out all the toxins from our body and find (feel that during breathe out all the toxins come out through our breathe).
- If we have time we can practise both *bhastrika* in the morning and evening.

Advantages

- *Bhastrika pranayama* increases the oxygen content in the blood. Extra oxygen replenishes the entire body.
- It removes blockages in the nose and chest.
- It is good for asthma patients and removes inflammation of the throat.
- *Bhastrika* increases the gastric fire and improves appetite.
- *Bhastrika* when practised with *kumbhaka* can generate heat in the body and keep it warm in cold weather.
- *Bhastrika* improves general health and activates all the organs.
- *Bhastrika* purifies the *nadis* (energy–pranic-channels) in the body, ensuring free flow of *prana* to all the organs in the body.
- *Bhastrika* has great spiritual benefits. It helps to break through the three *granthis* (psychic knots) that bind the soul. The three knots are called *brahma granthi* (at the base

of spine, near *muladhara* and *svadhishthana chakra*), *vishnu granthi* (around the heart *chakra*) and *rudra granthi* (at the *ajna chakra*). These are emotional and mental knots, blocking the individual's evolution. Prolonged practice of *bhastrika* loosens up these *granthis*. *Bhastrika* destroys the phlegm that blocks the entrance to *sushumna nadi* (or the central pranic channel), thus enabling energy to pass up the spinal channel. Prolonged practice can help to awaken the inherent *kundalini shakti* at the base of the spine.

- *Bhastrika* destroys the defects of *vata* (wind), *pitta* (bile) and *kapha* (phlegm) and balances these three.
- *Bhastrika pranayama* refreshes body and mind. It has a regenerating and rejuvenating influence upon the whole body and improves memory. Circulation is stimulated. The increased blood supply to the head improves eyesight and hearing. The lungs are strengthened and it is beneficial for bronchitis, as the respiratory system is quickly and deeply purified. Digestive function is stimulated, improving metabolism. The breakdown of fats is especially accelerated. This breathing technique also activates the solar plexus and *manipura chakra*.

Precautions

This *pranayama* should not be practised by people who are pregnant or have high blood pressure. Beginners should practise this *pranayama* slowly at first, allowing their bodies to adapt to the practice. Those suffering from heart diseases and fever should not do this *pranayama*. Also avoid it when one has a severe block in the nose. A person who had recent surgery, should consult his doctor before doing *bhastrika*. Practice of *bhastrika* can be little intense for some people. It should be learned only under the guidance of a qualified *yoga* instructor. In case of any existing medical conditions, one should consult his doctor before taking up the practice. Practice it at a slow pace in summer season. Those whose both nostrils are not properly open due to excess of cough or sinus problems, should first close the right nostril and do *rechaka* and *puraka* with left nostril. Then they should close the left nostril and do *rechaka* and *puraka* with the right nostril at slow, medium or vigorous speed as per their capacity. Then in the end, they should do *bhastrika pranayama* using both *ida* end *pingala* energy channels. One must practise this *pranayama* for 5 minutes daily. Keep the eyes closed while doing this *pranayama* and meditate on *om* in mind with each inhalation and exhalation.

KAPALABHATI PRANAYAMA

Kapala means "brain, forehead" and *bhati* means "glow, radiance, lustre, luminosity, etc." The *pranayama* which gives glow, radiance, lustre to the brain or forehead is called *kapalabhati*. The procedure of this *pranayama* is a bit different from *bhastrika*. In *rechaka* and *puraka* in the *bhastrika pranayama*, equal pressure is exerted on inhalation and exhalation, while in *kapalabhati* the whole attention is on *rechaka*, i.e. exhaling vigorously. No effort is made to breathe in, the air that is breathed in naturally is allowed to be inhaled; the whole emphasis is on throwing the air outside. While doing this there is naturally contraction and expansion of abdomen and special force is exerted on *muladhara* (pelvic plexus), *svadhishthana* (hypogastric plexus) and *manipura cakra* (solar plexus).

Noble Resolution

While doing *kapalabhati pranayama* one should resolve in mind that with the air exhaled by him all the diseases and disorders of the body are being thrown out, being eradicated. The *rechaka* (exhalation) procedure should be performed with the feeling that he is expelling all the physical diseases and disorders as well as the mental flaws and distortions like lust, anger, greed, delusion, envy, attachment and aversion. With this resolution of eradication of diseases and disorders while exhaling, one gets a lot of benefit.

Duration

The breath should be exhaled in a rhythmic flow once in a second and should be held up effortlessly.

If done non-stop *kapalabhati pranayama* is done 60 times in one minute or 300 times in 5 minutes. Very sick and weak persons get tired in 2-3 minutes in the beginning, but in 10-15 days every person becomes capable of doing *kapalabhati* non-stop for 5 minutes. *Kapalabhati* must be done for 5 minutes in one sitting. One cannot get full benefit of it if done for a lesser time. With the increase in capacity after a long practice as well as with the maturity of experience one can do *kapalabhati pranayama* up to 15 minutes. A healthy and even slightly sick person should do *kapalabhati* for 15 minutes. In three rounds in 15 minutes *kapalabhati* is done 900 times. Persons suffering from incurable diseases like cancer, AIDS, hepatitis, leucoderma, vitiligo, psoriasis, excessive obesity, infertility, cysts/nodules in uterus, ovary and breast or anywhere in the body, MS and SLE should do *kapalabhati* for half an hour. It would be better if such incurable patients do *kapalabhati* for half an hour both in the morning and evening. For healthy and slightly sick persons once a day is sufficient.

Advantages

- It increases glow, radiance, lustre and beauty of the face and brain.

- All *kapha* disorders like asthma, respiratory diseases, allergy and sinusitis are cured.
- All the diseases of heart, lungs and brain are cured.
- Obesity, diabetes, flatulence, constipation, acidity and kidney and prostate diseases are definitely cured.
- With the regular practice of this *pranayama* for about 5 minutes daily, an obstinate disease like constipation is cured. Diabetes can be regulated without any medicine and the weight due to abdominal fat can be reduced by 4-6 kg in one month. Blockages in the arteries of heart are removed.
- The mind remains stabilized, serene and cheerful. Negative thinking disappears and one gets rid of depression. The *chakra*s are cleansed and a divine energy starts circulating in all the *chakra*s, right from *muladhara chakra* (pelvic plexus) to *sahasrara chakra* (cerebral gland).
- This *pranayama* especially improves the health of stomach, pancreas, liver, spleen, intestines, prostate and kidneys. Even if one does not get much benefit by doing many *asana*s for stomach disorders, he can be benefited more than all the *asana*s by doing only this *pranayama*. This is the best *pranayama* for giving strength to weak intestines.

Practice

- Sit comfortably with the spine erect. Place hands on the knees, palms open to the sky.
- Take a deep breath in.
- Now exhale through both nostrils forcefully, so the stomach will go deep inside.
- As exhale, pull the stomach. Pull the navel back towards the spine. Do as much as one can. One may keep his right hand on the stomach to feel the abdominal muscles contract. Pull the navel in.
- As one relaxes the navel and abdomen, the breath flows into the lungs automatically.
- Take 20 such breaths to complete one round of *kapalabhati*

pranayama.

- Repeat this process for 5 minutes.
- After completing the round, relax with eyes closed and observe the sensations in the body.

Precautions

- One should avoid practising this breathing technique if he has an artificial pacemaker or stents, backache due to slip disc, recently went through an abdominal surgery, or is suffering from epilepsy or hernia.
- Women should not practise skull shining breathing technique (*kapalabhati pranayama*) during and shortly after pregnancy, as well as during menstruation as it involves vigorous abdominal squeezes.
- People with hypertension and heart problems should practise this breathing technique only under a *yoga* expert's guidance.

UJJAYI PRANAYAMA

In this *pranayama* we contract the throat while doing the *puraka* (inhaling) and when we breathe in by contracting the throat, we make a sound like snoring. We sit in a meditative pose and breathe in through both the nostrils. With some contraction of the throat we feel the friction of air in the throat. There should not be any friction of air in the nose. A sound is produced with the friction in the throat.

In the beginning we should practise only *puraka-rechaka* (inhaling-exhaling) without applying *kumbhaka* (holding in). After the *puraka* we should practise the *kumbhaka* gradually as long as the *puraka*, and after practising for some days we should double the duration of *kumbhaka*. If the *kumbhaka* is to be done for more than 10 seconds, we should apply *jalandhara bandha* and *mula bandha* as well. In this *pranayama* we should always do the *rechaka* exhaling) with the left nostril and keep the right nostril closed.

Advantages

This *pranayama* is beneficial for those who suffer from colds, cough and catarrh throughout the year, for those who suffer from thyroid problems, snoring, sleep apnoea, heart disease, asthma, lungs diseases, for those who suffer from throat problems like tonsilitis, thyroid glands, etc. and for those who suffer from insomnia, mental stress, hypertension, dyspepsia, rheumatism, dropsy, tuberculosis, fever, spleen disorders, etc. It should be practised regularly to keep the throat fit, healthy and melodious. It is an excellent *pranayama* for awakening *kundalini*, *ajapa-japa*, meditation, etc. It also rectifies the lispy (defective) speech of children.

ANULOMA-VILOMA PRANAYAMA

Practice

- Raise the right hand and with its thumb close the right nostril (*pingala nadi*) and while closing the left nostril use the ring finger and middle finger of the right hand.
- The palm of the hand should not be in front of the nose; it should instead be held away to the right side. Since *ida nadi* (left nostril) represents moon, lunar power, coolness and calmness, *anuloma-viloma pranayama* is started from the left nostril for cleansing the *nadi* (energy channel).
- Closing the right nostril with the right hand thumb, one should gently fill the breath inside through the left nostril.
- When the inhalation is complete, one should close the left

nostril with the ring finger and middle finger of the right hand and exhale completely through the right nostril.

- The rate of inhalation–exhalation should gradually be increased from medium to vigorous. Inhale vigorously with full force and then exhale. Make the rate of inhaling and exhaling slow, medium or fast according to one's capacity.
- If one does *puraka* (inhaling) and *rechaka* (exhaling) at a fast rate, there is a loud sound of breathing. After exhaled completely, keeping the left nostril closed, fill in complete breath through the right nostril and exhale it through the left nostril.
- Thus, one set is completed.
- One has to do this procedure non-stop, i.e. inhaling through the left nostril and exhaling through the right nostril, and then inhaling through the right nostril and exhaling through the left nostril.
- One starts feeling tired by repeating this series for one minute.
- When you feel tired, take some rest and begin the *pranayama* again when you feel better.

Thus one can begin this *pranayama* by doing for 3 minutes and it can go up to 10 minutes. After practising regularly for a few days the capacity of a learner starts increasing, and in about a week he can do this *pranayama* non-stop up to five minutes. With the constant practice of *anuloma-viloma* the energy lying in the *muladhara cakra* (pelvic plexus) starts awakening. Vedas call it being *urdhvaretas* (one with an upward movement of semen), and in the language of modern *yoga* it is known as *kundalini jagarana* (awakening of serpent energy). While doing this *pranayama* one should chant and meditate upon *om* in his mind with each inhalation–exhalation. By doing so, the mind gets situated in the sublime state of *dhyana* (meditation).

Noble Resolution

While doing this *pranayama*, one should think in his mind that with the friction and churning of breath in *ida* and *pingala nadis*, *sushumna nadi* is getting awakened. From the eight *chakras* right up to the *sahasrara chakra* (cerebral gland) a celestial light is moving upward. His whole body is aglow with a celestial light. One should meditate upon a celestial light, illumination and energy inside and outside the body, and realize *om kham brahma*. One should think that God, the controller of universe, is suffusing him with divine energy and divine knowledge. Initiate oneself into the discipline of *shaktipata* (instilling of energy). *Guru* (preceptor) is only a catalyst for attaining *shakti* (energy); he only connects one to divine vibrations. In fact, *shaktipata* is done by *om*, the Supreme Lord, the limitless ocean of energy. Thus, by practising this *anuloma-viloma pranayama*, by getting suffused with divine vibrations, one will be blessed with a lot of physical, mental and spiritual benefits. A light will stir up automatically from *muladhara chakra* (pelvic plexus), *kundalini* will awaken, one will become *urdhvaretas* (one with upward movement of semen) and will find oneself automatically suffused with divine energy.

Duration

- Filling in the breath with a rhythmic flow for about 2½ seconds through the left nostril, and without holding it up, throwing the breath out gently through the right nostril in about 2½ seconds, and immediately after throwing it out through the right nostril, filling in the breath effortlessly through the right nostril in 2½ seconds, and without holding it up, throwing it out in a rhythmic flow through the left nostril in about 2½ seconds. This procedure should be done non-stop for about 5 minutes, although it may be a bit tiresome in the beginning.

Precaution

- One set of *anuloma-viloma pranayama* will be performed in 10 seconds, i.e. 6 times in one minute. In a sitting of 5 minutes *anuloma-viloma* is performed about 30 times, and if a healthy person or a person suffering from light common ailments does it for the prescribed duration of 15 minutes, it will be performed in about 90 times.

- Persons suffering from incurable diseases like cancer, leucoderma/vitiligo, psoriasis, muscular dystrophy, SLE, infertility, HIV, AIDS, kidney diseases, etc. should practise *anuloma-viloma pranayama* up to 30 minutes.
- When the practice gets perfected *anuloma-viloma pranayama* can be done for 15 minutes or even half an hour at a stretch.

Advantages

- This *pranayama* cleanses 72,72,10,210 (seventy-two crore seventy-two lakh ten thousand two hundred ten) *nadi*s (energy channels). With the cleansing of all the *nadi*s the body becomes completely healthy, radiant and strong.
- All the *vata* diseases like arthritis, rheumatism, gout, Parkinson's disease and nervous debility, all *pitta* diseases like urinary diseases, tissue diseases, spermatorrhea, emissions, hyperacidity, heart burn and skin rashes, all *kapha* diseases like cold, catarrh, chronic rhinitis, sinusitis, asthma, cough, tonsils, etc. are cured. All the three *dosha*s are pacified.
- Blockages in the arteries of heart are removed. With the regular practice of this *pranayama*, almost 30-40 per cent blockages are removed in 3-4 months. We have tried it on a number of patients.
- All disorders of cholesterol, triglycerides, HDL, LDL, etc. are removed.
- Negative thinking is transformed into increasingly positive thinking. One starts attaining bliss, zest and fearlessness.
- In short, this *pranayama* purifies the body, the mind, the thoughts and the dispositions. All the diseases of the body are cured, and the mind is cleansed and gets absorbed in the meditation of *omkara*.
- By doing this *pranayama* 250-500 times, the serpent power (*kundalini shakti*) which lies with head downward in the pelvic

plexus (*muladhara chakra*) holds its head upward, and the process of *kundalini*-awakening sets in.

BHRAMARI PRANAYAMA

Practice

- Sit in any meditative posture.
- Inhale completely, press lightly at the root of the nose near the eyes with the middle fingers of both hands, keep the mind centred on the medullary plexus (*ajna chakra*).
- Close both the ears completely with thumbs. Now, humming like a bee and resonating *om*, breathe out. Repeat this procedure.

Noble Resolution

This *pranayama* should be done by identifying your consciousness with divine consciousness and God's existence. One should have in one's mind this divine resolution or thought that God's compassion, peace and bliss are raining on him. God is enriching him with pure intellect (*atambhara prajna*) by dispelling all his ignorance with His divine light illumining his *ajna chakra* (medullary plexus). Thus by doing this *pranayama* with pure intentions one feels a nebula of light in his *ajna chakra* and starts going into meditation automatically.

Duration

Inhaling for 3-5 seconds, and closing the ears, eyes, etc. as per the procedure, breathing it out in 15-20 seconds, makes one set of

bhramari pranayama. After completing one set, one should again breathe in for 3-5 seconds with a rhythmic flow, and humming like a bee breathe it out in 15-20 seconds according to procedure. Thus, everybody should do *bhramari pranayama* at least 5-7 times non-stop, which will take about 3 minutes. Those who are suffering from cancer, depression, Parkinson's disease, migraine, heart disease and some other incurable disease or who are desirous of fathoming the depths of *yoga* can do *bhramari pranayama* 11-21 times.

Advantages

It dispels the instability/fickleness of mind and is beneficial in mental tension, agitation, high BP, heart disease, etc. It is very useful for meditation.

BAHYA PRANAYAMA

- Sit properly in *siddhasana* or *padmasana* and throw the breath out, as much as one can, in one go.
- After throwing the breath out, apply *mula bandha*, *uddiyana bandha* and *jalandhara bandha*, and hold the breath out as much as possible.
- When one feels like breathing in, take the breath while relaxing the *bandhas* slowly.
- After taking in the breath, throw it out again as before, without holding it up.

Noble Resolution

Like *kapalabhati*, in this *pranayama* also all the disorders and *doshas* are being expelled while breathing out, this is what we should say to ourselves. We should know it for certain that the stronger is our power of thinking, the sooner will disappear all our afflictions. If our mind is inspired by a noble resolution, all our mental and physical diseases will be eradicated and we will be benefited all over.

Duration

Filling in the breath effortlessly in 3-5 seconds, throwing it out effortlessly in 3-5 seconds, holding it out for 10-15 seconds, and again filling it in 3-5 seconds and doing *bahya pranayama* by exhaling it, in this way *bahya pranayama* is completed in about 20-25 seconds. It is better if two *bahya pranayamas* are done non-stop one after the other. If in the beginning one has to take 1-2 normal breaths between two *pranayamas*, one may take them. Normally one can easily do *bahya pranayama* 5 times in 2 minutes, and that is generally sufficient. Persons suffering from rectal prolapsed, piles, fissure, fistula, vaginal prolapsed, excessive urination, scanty urination and venereal diseases can practise it up to 11 times. Seekers desirous of awakening *kundalini* and of being *urdhvaretas* (with upward movement of semen) may practise it maximum 21 times.

Advantages

- It is a harmless *pranayama*. It dispels the instability of mind.
- It improves the digestive power and is beneficial in stomach ailments.
- It makes the intellect sharp and subtle.
- It cleanses the body. By promoting the upward movement of semen, it removes the sexual disorders like nocturnal emissions, quick ejaculation, etc.
- In *bahya pranayama* all the organs in the abdomen are strained a lot and slight pain is felt in the weak or diseased part of the abdomen in the beginning. Therefore, for giving some relaxation and therapy to the abdomen, this *pranayama* should be done by applying the three *bandhas*.

Precautions

People with hypertension and heart problem should avoid performing *bahya pranayama*.

UDGITHA PRANAYAMA

Inhale for 3-5 seconds in a rhythmic flow, and breathe it out in about 15-20 seconds while chanting the sacred word *om* methodically. After one chanting is complete one should again breathe deep inside for 3-5 seconds in a rhythmic flow and breathe it out in 15-20 seconds chanting *om*. Thus, everybody must do *udgitha pranayama* about 7 times in about 3 minutes. Those who are suffering from incurable diseases and the learners (*sadhakas*) desirous of fathoming the depths of meditation can do *udgitha pranayama* for 5-10 minutes or even longer. Both *bhramari* and *udgitha* are gentle and effortless *pranayamas*. Therefore, if a *sadhaka* practises them for longer duration there is no possibility of any sort of harm.

PRANAVA PRANAYAMA

After doing all the *pranayamas*, concentrate your mind on inhalation and exhalation, and meditate upon *udgitha* (*om*) with your *prana*. God has made poles in the shape of *omkara*. This *pinda* (body) and this *brahmanda* (universe) both are in the form of *omkara*. *Omkara* is not a particular person or figure; it is a divine power which is controlling and regulating the whole universe. Turn yourself into a spectator (= soul) and while inhaling deeply and exhaling subtly your respiration rate should be so subtle that you do not feel like hearing the sound of your breath, and even if one puts a cotton swab before your nose it should not shake or quiver. Gradually increase the practice and try to breathe in and breathe out once in one minute.

Thus, try to look at the breath inside. In the beginning the friction of breath will be felt on the tip of nose. Gradually you shall be able to feel the touch of breath deep inside you. Thus, by chanting *omkara* with every breath as a spectator (= soul), one starts going into meditation automatically. Your mind will become highly one-pointed, absorbed in and identified with *omkara*. Along with *pranava* the great Gayatri Mantra from the Vedas should be chanted and recited, imbibing its meaning. Thus, through meditation a seeker can become identified with *Brahman*, the very essence of existence, consciousness and bliss, and can attain the unique divine ecstasy of *samadhi*. Even while going to bed one should meditate into sleep. By doing so his sleep will be blessed with *yoga*; he will get rid of nightmares and will have a quick and sound sleep.

Duration

When as a spectator (= soul) we concentrate our mind on the rhythmic flow of breaths, the *prana* gets subtle automatically, and we inhale once in 10-20 seconds and exhale in 10-20 seconds. Through long practice a *yogi* takes one breath in one minute. After *bhastrika, kapalabhati, bahya, anuloma-viloma, bhramari* and *udgitha*, this *pranava pranayama* is done, which is another form of *vipashyana* or *preksha dhyana.* It is completely meditation based. Everybody must do this meditation-based *pranayama. Yogis* practising *samadhi* do this penance of breathing accompanied with meditation of *pranava* for hours together, according to the availability of time. There is no sound of breathing in this procedure, i.e. this soundless penance takes a seeker into the deep silence within, where his senses merge with the mind, the mind with the *prana* and the *prana* with the soul, and through soul a seeker realizes the universal supreme soul, *Brahman.* It is the path which has *pranayama* as its starting point from where it gradually and spontaneously leads from the constant practice of *pranayama* to *pratyahara* (withdrawal), from the constant practice of *pratyahara* to *dharana* (concentration), from the firm and constant practice of *dharana* to *dhyana* (meditation) and from the constant practice of *dhyana* to *samadhi* (absorption). With this *prana-sadhana* (*pranayama*), there is a union of *dharana, dhyana* and *samadhi*, and *sanyama* is attained (*trayamekatra sanyama*). From *sanyama* a *sadhaka* attains *prajnaloka*, which gives himself healing, which ultimately blesses him with the experience of self-realization.

He is encompassed by a dazzling aura which works as an impenetrable armour to protect the *sadhaka* (seeker) from all diseases, disorders and polluting influences.

SURYABHEDA PRANAYAMA

Suryabhedana pranayama or *suryabheda pranayama* is very effective *pranayama* which is mentioned in *Hatha-Yoga Pradipika*. The meaning of *surya* is sun and the meaning of the word *bhedana* is piercing, enter or breaking through something. In *yoga* terminology right *nadi* (right nostril) is called *surya nadi* or *pingala*, and left *nadi* (left nostril) is called *chandra nadi* or *ida nadi*. The right *nadi* is the entrance way of *pingala nadi*, speaking to the sun vitality, the hot vitality or the manly vitality in our body. It is the vitality which is in charge of animation and physical work. By practising *suryabhedana pranayama* we are seriously initiating the sun vitality or as it were activating so as to make a leap forward of sun vitality the right nostril relaxing. *Yoga* propounds that in our body the place of sun is close to the navel and also the moon within the skull. Whereas the moon contains a cooling result, and the sun creates heating impact. In this process we use right *nadi* (right nostril) to breathe in (inhalation) and the left nostril to breathe out.

Practice

- Sit in *padmasana* or any comfortable *asana*.
- Close the eyes.
- Keep the left nostril closed with your right ring and little fingers.
- Slowly inhale without making any sound as long as you can do it comfortably through the right nostril.
- Then close the right nostril with your right thumb and retain the breath firmly pressing the chin against the chest (*jalandhara bandha*). You will have to increase the period of *kumbhaka* gradually.
- The one round is now complete.
- Repeat this pose in the same manner 3 to 5 times.

Precautions

- If you feel little bit of discomfort, you can reduce the ratio of breathing.
- Under no circumstances the proportion of the breathing should be forced.
- People who have undergone abdominal surgeries, heart

surgeries, brain surgeries should consult the medical expert before starting with this *pranayama.*

Advantages

- *Suryabheda pranayama* activates the body and the bodily functions.
- It increases the digestive fire. It destroys all diseases that are caused by insufficiency of oxygen in the blood.
- *Gheranda Samhita* says that *suryabheda pranayama* destroys decay and death, awakens *kundalini shakti* and increases digestive fire.
- *Hatha-Yoga Pradipika* says that *suryabheda pranayama* cleans the frontal sinuses, destroys disorders of *vata* and destroys intestinal worms.
- In *Hatha-Yoga Pradipika,* it is also said that one can perform *uddiyana bandha* by pulling in the abdomen at the end of *kumbhaka* or holding of breath. This will force the *prana* to enter the central pranic channel called *sushumna nadi.* This leads to awakening of the *kundalini shakti.*

CHANDRABHEDA PRANAYAMA

The word *chandra* stands for the moon and the meaning of *bhedana* is piercing, enter or breaking through something, etc. and it is also known as *chandrabheda pranayama.* It is a simple and effective breathing technique. In this breathing exercise breathe in (inhalation) is done by the left *nadi* (left nostril) and breathe out through the right *nadi* (right nostril). So this process is named as left nostril breathing. It is said that energy passes through *ida nadi* (*chandra nadi*) on the inhalation and by *pingala* (*surya nadi*) on the exhalation. These are larger *nadi*s that hold the balance of magnetism and energy created by the sun and moon.

Practice

- Choose a comfortable sitting *asana* like *svastikasana* or *padmasana* and sit comfortably.

- Now use your right thumb to shut the right nostril. (If you are left handed then make the *pranayama-mudra* with your left hand and shut the right nostril with index and middle finger of your left hand.)
- Now inhale slowly and deeply through your left *nadi* until your lungs fills with maximum air.
- Now hold your breath for some time or as per your capacity.
- Breathe out (exhale) slowly through right *nadi.* (Exhalation should be longer than the inhalation.)
- Repeat this process around 3-5 times.

Advantages

- Helpful in reducing the body heat.
- When the inhalation is done through the left nostril, your body gets cooled.
- It reduces the bile and removes the excess heat of the body. You do not feel tired and belching is stopped.
- Refreshes the body and mind and kicks out the feeling of laziness.
- Very effective in high blood pressure.
- Useful in fever.
- Mind becomes steady by the daily practice of this *pranayama.*
- Useful in reducing the tension, stress and other mental problems.

Precautions

Do not perform *chandrabhedana pranayama* in case of *asthma*, low blood pressure, cough and cold and problems related to respiratory system.

SHEETALI PRANAYAMA (COOLING BREATH)

Sheetali in Sanskrit means "cooling". *Sheetali pranayama* is mentioned in the *yoga* texts *Hatha-Yoga Pradipika* and *Gheranda Samhita.* The meaning of word *sheetali* is cooling down, that process which can

cool down our body and gives feeling of coolness. The daily practice of *sheetali pranayama* can calm the mind along with body.

Practice

- Sit comfortably in any meditative pose like *padmasana* and *svastikasana.*
- Keep your both hands on knees.
- Open your mouth and stretch your tongue outside the lips.
- Fold the tongue like a pipe from both the sides.
- Inhale gently, not forcefully, through the folded tongue with opened eyes (good for eyes) with the hissing sound like . . . *sh* . . . *sh* . . . *sh* and feel the coolness at the back of the throat.
- Then take the tongue inside your mouth and close the lips firmly.
- Hold the breath as long as possible with closed eyes.
- Very very slowly exhale through the nose without opening your mouth and feel the coolness of the breath penetrating into the brain and spreading out into your entire nervous system.
- This is one round. Make 5-10 rounds like this.

- The *sheetali pranayama* can be practised for 20-30 minutes without any side effect or any other complication.

Advantages

- The action of pulling the air through the tongue creates a cooling effect on the body.
- *Sheetali* relaxes the body and mind.
- According to *Hatha-Yoga Pradipika*, *sheetali* can cure colic, enlarged spleen, fever and disorders of the bile. *Sheetali* can also remove hunger and thirst.
- *Gheranda Samhita* describes *sheetali* as the giver of bliss. The text says that *sheetali* removes indigestion, phlegm and bilious disorders.
- The practice of *sheetali pranayama* before sunrise increases memory and intelligence. This *pranayama* refreshes the body, mind and purifies the blood.
- Those people who feel tired, lazy and sleepy while getting up in the morning or even during the day, must practise this *pranayama*. The basic purpose of the *sheetali pranayama* is to decrease or cool down the body temperature, this may have positive impact on our nervous system and endocrine glands. Person becomes young and charming by practising this process which is mentioned in *Hatha-Yoga Pradipika* by Swami Swatmarama.

Precautions

Avoid this *pranayama* in extreme cold weather. Also avoid if having cold, cough, asthma, tuberculosis, breathing problem, lung disorder, arthritis, low blood pressure or chronic constipation problems.

SHEETKARI PRANAYAMA

Sheetkari means the breathing technique that "produces the '*seee*' or the '*seet* (hissing)' sound". *Sheetkari* is a variation of *sheetali pranayama*.

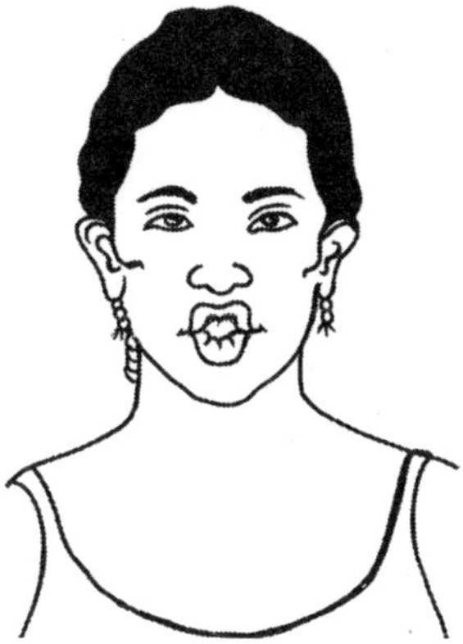

Practice

- Sit in any meditative posture.
- Open the lips and fold the tongue inward towards the throat.
- Touch the tip of the tongue against the upper palate.
- Keep the upper and lower teeth together.
- Inhale deeply and gently through the teeth with opened eyes with a sound like . . . *sh* . . . *sh* . . . *sh* and feel the coolness at the back of the throat.
- Then keep the lips closed and relax the tongue.
- Hold the breath as long as you can, with closed eyes. Slowly, slowly exhale through the nose without opening the mouth and feel the coolness of the breath into your entire nervous system and the mind.
- This is one round. Make 5-10 rounds like this.
- The practice of *sheetkari pranayama* can be done for 20-30 minutes.

Advantages

The same as we have in the practice of *sheetali pranayama.*

Both the *pranayamas* have same benefits. In addition, *sheetkari* keeps the mouth clean and cool, good for teeth, gums and cures pyorrhoea.

Precautions

Persons with high blood pressure may find greater strain in *sheetkari* than in *sheetali pranayama.*

Some Other Pranayamas[9]

Yugrishi Shriram Sharma Acharya has recommended the following *pranayamas* for the physical, mental and spiritual well-being of the aspirants.

PRANAKARSHAN PRANAYAMA

In this *pranayama* the aspirant attracts, draws and absorbs the pranic/cosmic energy.

Practice

- In the early pre-dawn hours after performing daily ablutions sit cross-legged facing the eastern direction.
- Place both hands on the knees. Close your eyes. Meditate on the fact that in the entire sky *prana* principle, full of light and energy, pervades it.
- Imagine that *prana,* akin to clouds of hot steam shining in sun light, is flowing towards us from all directions. And within this *prana* we are seated contented, peaceful and joyful.
- From both nostrils start inhaling and meditate on the fact that we are imbibing within the body clouds of *prana* principle. Just as a bird and snake enter their nest and hole in the same way scattered *prana* that flows around us is entering our body via the nose. Thus it is also entering our brain, chest, heart, stomach and all other organs.
- When you inhale deeply stop it from getting exhaled for some time and feel mentally: The *prana* I have inhaled is now pervading every pore of my body. Just as when you pour water on mud it soaks the water so too our bodily parts are like dry mud and water as *prana* is being soaked by our entire

[9] http://www.Sriramsharma.com

body. Further our body is also fully imbibing consciousness, divine light, strength, zest, enterprise, patience and valour that are conjoined to *prana* (vital force).

- Try and stop exhalation (after inhaling air) as long as you are comfortable and then slowly exhale. At that time mentally think: After imbibing the essence of *prana* in every pore of my body dirty air is being emitted out of the body. It is like throwing away remnants after butter is churned from buttermilk. All mental taints and distortions are being emitted via exhalation and like black smoke it is throwing out all unwholesome imprints of the psyche.
- After exhaling fully let the air remain outside for some time. Meaning live without air for some time and think: Since all the taints of my mind have been exhaled I will shut all doors on them. Now these distortions have run away miles from me.
- Before doing *japa* (*mantra* chanting) daily perform this *prana-karshan pranayama* classified in five parts. Initially perform five rounds of this *pranayama*. After this every month increase the number by one more round of *pranayama*. After increasing thus in one year you should be able to do it for half an hour.

LOMA–VILOMA SURYAVEDHANA PRANAYAMA

Prana pulled within via inhalation of air is awakening the solar plexus in the navel region. It pierces its lethargy and dark gloominess. From there via the *sushumna* path this radiance travels to the stomach, chest and throat. Hence this *pranayama* is called *suryavedhana*. *Loma* means straight and *viloma* means upside down. Once straight–once upside down. Then upside down and then straight. Then upside down, inhaling from left, emitting from right. Inhaling from right and exhaling from left. Because of this cycle of straight/upside down it is called *loma–viloma suryavedhana pranayama*.

Practice

- In a peaceful lonely area be seated with balanced pose. Face the east, sit cross-legged, sit in the easy lotus posture, spine should be erect, eyes must be half shut, place hands on both knees. This is called the *prana-mudra* and be seated thus.
- Bend the left hand and keep it slanting. In its palms place the elbow of the right hand. Raise the right hand. Place the thumb on the right nostril and place the middle and ring finger on the left nostril.
- Close the left nostril with the help of the middle and ring finger. When you inhale air it must not be spread out in the lungs merely but should also go to your navel area. Slowly allow the air to fill up the stomach comfortably.
- Meditate on the fact that the sun's light on mixing with air enters the body via the *pingala* subtle nerve situated in the right nostril. Its heat is radiating our inner body organs.
- Let the inhaled air remain for some time inside. Shut both the nostrils and meditate on the fact that via the concentrated light of *prana* of *nabhi* (navel), *chakra* (subtle plexus) is getting focused in the navel subtle plexus. The solar plexus having remained latent for a long time in the navel is now being influenced by this concentrated *prana* light. Hence it is becoming radiant and its aura is continuously augmenting.
- Now shut the right nostril with the thumb. Open the left nostril. Slowly exhale air from the left nostril. Now meditate on the fact that the dirt that induces inactivation in the *chakras* is being emitted totally. Now since this dirt is mixed with the exhaled air it is no longer radiant as it was when vital force was inhaled. It is hence becoming yellow in colour and via the *ida* subtle nerve it is being emitted from the left nostril's exhaled air. Now close both the nostrils. Render the lungs empty, i.e. devoid of air. Meditate that the external vital force remains outside only. Since it does not pressurize the internal vital force it is very light in weight.

The *prana* of the *nabhi chakra* is focused like the sun. Like a ball of light it rises upwards as fire flames. Its flames travel from the upper region of the stomach to the throat. In the inner subtle *sushumna* nerve this ball of fire (vital force) is making the internal body radiant.

- With the thumb close the right nostril and inhale air from the left nostril. Think that via the *ida* subtle nerve *prana* shining brilliantly like the sun and mixed in air is entering the body. This light is entering the solar plexus situated in the navel along the spine (*merudanda*). There it is getting focused. Due to the focus of this radiant light the solar plexus or *surya chakra* is becoming more radiant.
- Now shut both the nostrils. Stop the air from flowing out of the body. Meditate that radiant *prana* mixed with inhaled air is entering the navel's solar plexus and is rendering it permanently radiant. The radiance keeps augmenting and like tongues of flames is marching upwards. Because of this light the *sushumna* subtle nerve is getting nourished ceaselessly.
- Close the left nostril and from the right nostril slowly exhale air. Meditate that the dirt of *surya chakra* like smoke mixed with radiant breath is rendering the latter opaque and yellow. This yellow *prana* air is being evicted outside via the *pingala* subtle nerve. Now since the inner dirt has been removed the psyche/heart feels light and radiant.
- Now again shut both the nostrils and render the lungs empty, i.e. devoid of any air. Feel the ball of light of *sushumna* subtle nerve going upward from *nabhi chakra* to the throat. Experience that divine brilliant light shines in the inner bodily parts.

NADI-SHODHANA PRANAYAMA (PURIFICATION OF NADIS)

Practice

- In pre-dawn hours facing the east, with spine erect sit cross-legged. Keep the eyelids half shut.

- Close the right nostril. Inhale air from the left nostril and keep on pulling it till the *nabhi chakra.*
- Meditate on the fact that in the navel area is present the full moon-like cool light. The inhaled air is touching it.
- Stop the breath from going out for as long as you had inhaled it. Meditate that the inhaled air which touched the cool full moon-like light of *nabhi chakra* is itself becoming cool and radiant.
- Now exhale air from the same nostril from which you inhaled air. Meditate that the air (exhalation) which has become cool and radiant on touching the *nabhi chakra* is making the *ida* subtle nerve (from which it is exhaled) cool and radiant while exhaling.
- For some time let the exhaled air remain outside (do not inhale) and again start the above-mentioned process through left nostril. Close the right nostril with the right thumb. Do this cycle three times.
- Just as you have done *puraka, kumbhaka, rechaka, bahya kumbhaka* from the left nostril in the same way do it from the right nostril. In the *nabhi chakra* meditate on the sun instead of the moon. While exhaling think that the air being exhaled while touching the sun in the navel is rendering the breathing tube warm and radiant.
- While closing the left nostril, perform the above action three times.
- Now open both nostrils. Inhale air simultaneously from both nostrils and do not let it go out (do not exhale). While opening the mouth exhale air from it. This action should be carried out only once.

Three times while inhaling and exhaling from the left nostril meditate on the cool radiant moon on the *nabhi chakra.* Three times while inhaling and exhaling from the right nostril meditate on the warm radiant sun on the *nabhi chakra.* Once inhale from both nostrils, shut the nostrils and exhale slowly from the mouth. All these seven steps put together makes one *nadi-shodhana pranayama* (yogic subtle nerve purification).

Advantages

After practising the above the aspirant (*sadhaka*) will get divine experiences. This can be demonstrated to a trustworthy person. Guidance too can be asked for but never should this be used for idle superficial information and talk. If these *pranayama*s have matured then on the basis of experiences attained so far further guidance can be taken.

Precaution

- Practise *pranayama* on an empty stomach.
- The place should be pure and full of fresh air. Never practise *pranayama* where there is stench.
- Initially perform only one or two *pranayama*s and only later increase time and number.
- After performing *pranayama,* do not lift heavy objects for one hour.

Bandhas

Bandha means to hold, tighten, lock, close-off or stop. The *bandha*s aim to lock the *prana*s in particular areas and redirect their flow into *sushumna nadi* for the purpose of spiritual awakening. When the *bandha* is released, this causes the energy to flow more strongly through the locked part with an increased pressure.

There are four types of *bandha*s:

- *Mula bandha* (anal lock)
- *Uddiyana bandha* (lifting of the diaphragm)
- *Jalandhara bandha* (chin lock)
- *Maha bandha* (practice of all the *bandha*s together).

Generally, the breath is held during the practice of *bandhas*. *Mula bandha* and *jalandhara bandha* can be performed after the inhalation as well as after the exhalation. *Uddiyana bandha* and *maha bandha* are only performed after the exhalation.

The three *bandhas* – *mula bandha, uddiyana bandha* and *jalandhara bandha* – directly act on the three *granthi*s (psychic knots). *Mula bandha* is associated with *brahma granthi, uddiyana bandha* with *vishnu granthi* and *jalandhara bandha* with *rudra granthi*. The *granthi*s prevent the free flow of *prana* along the *sushumna nadi* and thus impede the awakening of the *chakra*s and the rising of *kundalini*.[10]

Brahma granthi is the first knot and is associated with *muladhara* and *svadhishthana chakras*. It is linked with the survival instinct, the urge to procreate. When *brahma granthi* is transcended, the *kundalini* (primal energy) is able to rise beyond *muladhara* and *svadhishthana* without being pulled back down by the attractions and instinctual patterns of the personality.

The second knot is *vishnu granthi*, associated with *manipura* and *anahata chakras*. These two *chakra*s are associated with the sustenance of the physical, emotional and mental aspects of human existence. Once *vishnu granthi* is transcended, energy is drawn from the universe and not from the localized centres within the human being. The final knot is *rudra granthi* which is associated with *vishuddhi* and *ajna chakras*. *Vishuddhi* and *ajna* sustain the intuitive or higher mental body and represent the transformation of an existing form, idea or concept into its universal aspect. When *rudra granthi* is pierced, individuality is dropped, the old ego awareness is left behind and the experience of unmanifest consciousness emerges beyond *ajna chakra* at *sahasrara*.[11]

Adi Shankaracharya says that *jalandhara bandha, mula bandha, uddiyana bandha* and *maha bandha* are situated respectively, in the throat, abdomen and perineum. If their duration can be increased, where is the fear of death?[12]

---

[10] Saraswati, 2002, *Asana, Pranayama, Mudra, Bandha*, p. 407.

[11] Ibid., p. 408.

[12] *Yogaratnavali* (*sutra* 5; Sri Adi Shankaracharya).

MULA BANDHA

- Awareness: on the *muladhara chakra.*
- Breathing: inhale deeply and hold the breath, *mula bandha* may also be performed with external breath retention.
- Repetitions: 3-5 rounds.

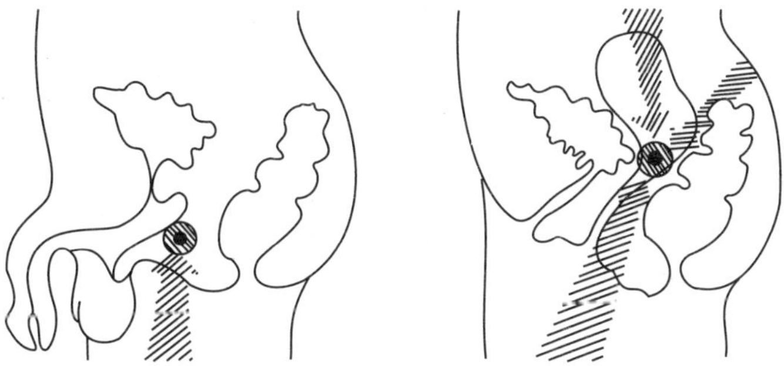

Practice

- Sit in a meditation *asana* like *siddhasana* which presses the heel into the perineum.
- Place the palms on the knees.
- Close the eyes and relax the body for a few minutes.
- Inhale deeply and hold the breath.
- Perform *mula bandha* by slowly contracting the perineal/ vaginal region and hold the contraction as tightly as possible. Do not strain.
- Concentrate on the *muladhara chakra* and firmly contract the anal muscles.
- Hold it for as long as the breath can comfortably be retained.
- Slowly release *mula bandha*, raise the head to the upright position and exhale.

Advantages

It strengthens the pelvic floor muscles, relieves haemorrhoids and congestion in the pelvic area. *Mula bandha* calms the autonomic nervous system, calms and relaxes the mind. On the spiritual level, it activates and purifies the *muladhara chakra*. It awakens dormant consciousness and the *kundalini shakti.*

UDDIYANA BANDHA

- Awareness: on the *manipura chakra.*
- Breathing: completely exhale and hold the breath out.
- Repetitions: 3-5 rounds.

Practice

- Sit in a meditative *asana.*
- Completely exhale and hold the breath out.
- Place the palms on the knees.
- Close the eyes and relax the whole body. Breath in deeply through both the nostrils.
- Exhale through the mouth with a whoosh, emptying the lungs as much as possible.
- Hold the breath outside.
- Lean forward and press down on the knees with the palms.
- Straighten the elbows and raise the shoulders and tilt the body forward slightly, pressing the chin against the chest.
- Concentrate on the *manipura chakra*, pull the abdominal muscles in and up into the abdominal cavity as far as possible. Hold the position as long as comfortable.
- Release the muscular tension and return to the starting position with a deep inhalation.

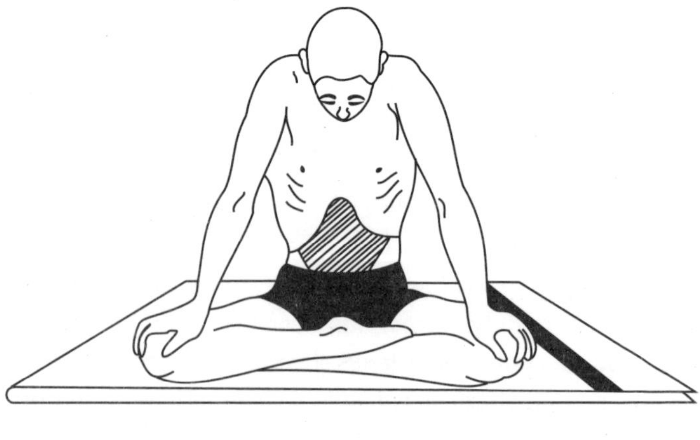

- Breathing normally remains for some time in this position.

Advantages

Uddiyana bandha activates the *manipura chakra* and solar plexus. It stimulates intestinal activity, helps relieve constipation, stimulates the pancreas and is helpful for diabetes. It also strengthens the immune system, balances the mind, soothes irritability and anger, and dispels a depressive mood.

Precaution

Perform only on an empty stomach. Do not practise this *bandha* if one has high blood pressure, stomach or intestinal ulcer or heart disease. Pregnant women should avoid it.

JALANDHARA BANDHA

- Awareness: on the *vishuddhi chakra.*
- Breath: inhale deeply and hold the breath.
- Repetitions: 3-5 rounds.

Practice

- Sit in a meditation pose.
- Place the hands on the knees.

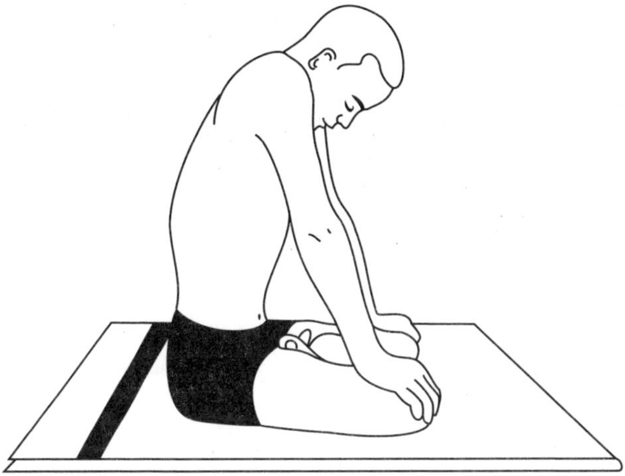

- Close the eyes and relax the whole body.
- Inhale deeply and hold the breath.
- Lift the shoulders and tilt the body forward slightly, keeping the back straight.
- Press the chin firmly against the chest or between the collarbones so that the windpipe and oesophagus are firmly closed.
- Concentrate on the *vishuddhi chakra* and hold the breath for as long as comfortable. Raise the head and with a long exhalation return to the starting position.
- Breathe normally and remain in this position for some time.

Advantages

This *bandha* awakens the inner energy centres, especially the *vishuddhi chakra.* It Improves the ability to retain the breath for a long period of time and develops the ability to concentrate. Beneficial for throat diseases, it regulates the thyroid function.

Precaution

The breath should only be held for as long as easily possible. People suffering from cervical spondylosis, high intracranial pressure, vertigo, high blood pressure or heart disease should not practise *jalandhara bandha.*

MAHA BANDHA

- Awareness: on the *muladhara, manipura* and *vishuddhi chakras.*
- Breathing: exhale completely and hold the breath.
- Repetitions: 3-5 rounds.

Practice

- Sit in any meditation posture.
- Place the palms on the knees.
- Close the eyes and relax the whole body. Breath in deeply through the nostrils.
- Now inhale deeply and exhale fully through the mouth.

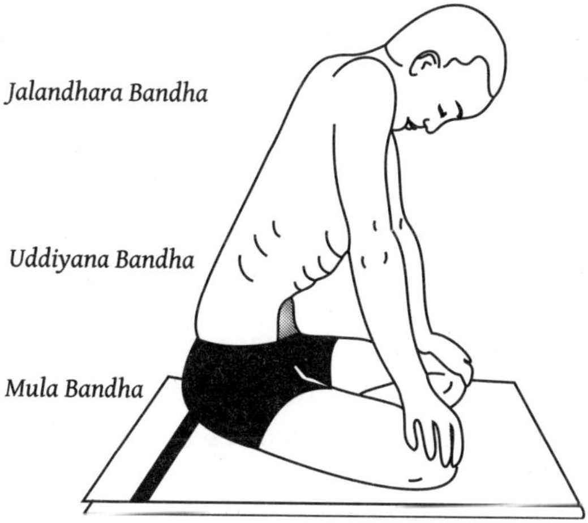

Maha Bhanda

- Hold the breath out.
- Simultaneously perform the three *bandhas*, i.e. *jalandhara bandha* (chin lock), then *uddiyana bandha* (abdominal lock) and then the *mula bandha* (root lock) in that order. Retain the breath outside.
- Retaining the breath outside is called *bahir kumbhaka.* Retain the breath outside for as long as you are comfortable. During retention, awareness can be maintained on any of the three *chakras* – *muladhara, manipura* and *vishuddhi.*
- To release the *maha bandha,* first release *mula bandha* (root lock), then the *uddiyana bandha* (abdominal lock) and then finally the *jalandhara bandha* (chin lock) in that order.
- This is one round of *maha bandha.* Repeat the process for as many times as you feel comfortable. Take ample rest after each round by doing relaxed breathing till you are ready for the next round.

Advantages

- Beneficial for the health of the whole body, especially the autonomic nervous system, internal organs, muscles and nerves.

- *Maha bandha* gives the combined benefits of all the three basic *bandhas* – *mula, uddiyana* and *jalandhara.*
- It also activates the three *chakras* – *muladhara, manipura* and *vishuddhi.*
- It activates the pineal glands and therefore regulates the entire endocrine glands.
- It rejuvenates the cells in the entire body and hence helps as an anti-ageing mechanism.
- During initial stages there is discomfort to retain the breath. But with practice, breath can be retained for long durations. When the lock is released, there is a general sense of well-being and bliss. The mind calms down and there is experience of a peaceful state. It removes the afflictions of the mind like anger and lust.
- *Maha bandha* is practised by *yogis* to attain a peaceful and introverted state of mind before starting the practice of meditation.
- The practice of *maha bandha*, pulls the pranic energy upwards. The *apana vayu* is pulled up and merges with the *prana vayu* in the abdominal region, which is the seat of *samana vayu.* This awakens the *prana shakti* which brings about heightened levels of awareness. With practice it will awaken the *kundalini shakti* resting at the base of the spine as well.
- *Gheranda Samhita* and *Hatha-Yoga Pradipika* describe *maha bandha* as the conqueror of old age and death. Also, all the desires of the *yogi* is fulfilled by practising this *bandha.*

Precaution

Maha bandha should not be practised by those suffering from blood pressure problems, heart diseases, ulcer of stomach or intestine, stroke, paralysis and hernia. Also pregnant women should avoid this practice.

Trataka (Yogic Gazing)

The term *trataka* means intent gazing, looking at an object intensely.

Trataka is not a simple look, but intense look at some object. In Sanskrit it is known as *drishti*. *Trataka* is of two kinds: internal and external. Internal *trataka* is called *dharana* (concentration) because in this practice the eyes are closed and the mind is concentrated upon some subtle element within. External *trataka* means fixing the eyes on some object outside. *Bahiranga trataka* is easier to practise because one simply has to gaze at an object or a symbol. However, *antaranga trataka* involves clear and stable inner visualization of an object. In the practice of *trataka* an object is gazed at until its subtle form manifests in front of the closed eyes. The point of concentration is usually a symbol or object which activates the inner potential and can absorb the mind.

Trataka is gazing without blinking at an object placed directly in front of the eyes. At the time of practising *trataka*, the eyeballs should remain steady and the eyelids should not flicker. No object except the one on which *trataka* is to be performed should be seen, and the mind should not wander hither and thither but be merged in observation of the object. *Trataka* on any object can be performed during the day or night. In this practice one has to take into account the object, the place and the time. What is the object on which the eyes are to be fixed? Where is the object to be placed? At what time should it be practised?

PREPARATION FOR PRACTICE

- Sit in any meditation or comfortable posture.
- Back and neck must be erect.
- Select and practise any method of *trataka*, according to your choice as mentioned below.
- Practise daily with regularity at same place and time.
- Keep negative thoughts and lust away from your mind.
- Do *trataka* with dedication, patience and concentration.
- Gradually, increase the time from 5 minutes to about 30 minutes.
- *Brahma muhurta* (4 a.m. to 6 a.m.) is the ideal time for

practising *trataka*. It bestows divine results very soon.

- We must achieve peace of mind before starting *trataka* for wonderful and suitable result. Hence, practising *pranayama* before *trataka* is of great help and contributes a lot to the *sadhana*.

PRACTICE OF TRATAKA

There are many methods of *trataka* which can be practised by aspirants/*sadhaka*s according to choice and situation. Swami Satyananda Saraswati has recommended some specific practices for the aspirants. Some of them are as follows.

On Candle Flame

Light a candle in the darkness and fix your eyes on the flame for 5 or 10 minutes without blinking. The candle should be an arm's length from the body. Perform this practice in the morning and evening. There should be no break even for a day in this *sadhana*. It should continue as long as the eyes cannot fix themselves steadily on the flame. People with eye defects should practise this *sadhana*. Even children who suffer from eye defects should be encouraged to practise this technique.

How to Practise Trataka on a Candle Light?: You should have a steady stand and on that the candle is to be placed. Place it in a room where the breeze is not blowing and where it is absolutely calm and quiet. When the flame becomes steady, you should look into the flame without winking. Do not look into the whole flame, but into the centre part of the flame, as long as possible, but without winking and without strain. Tears should not roll down. No strain at all. Then close your eyes. The moment you close your eyes, look within practise *trataka* on internal psychic point. Here a combination with *trataka* on external objects and *trataka* on internal psychic point is made. Close your eyes and look somewhere here in *chidakasha* and you will find a small, tiny, luminous, coloured, dot manifesting. Look at the dot. It is something like a small piece of wheat, paddy, barley.

Something of the same colour and shape, but the colour changes from moment to moment. It depends on how long you have done the gaze. When you have done it for 5 minutes it will be bright red. But when you have looked at the candle light for 1 minute, it will be just something the psychic consciousness, and recollect that psychic point and in a few seconds the same thing will reappear. And when it reappears it will have a different colour altogether. You keep looking at it with the help of your inner vision, eyes, inner sense, sense of perception. It will again grow dim, fainter, faintest and still faintest and it will disappear. Still do not open your eyes, but assemble your consciousness again recollecting that particular point and see it comes once again before your vision. And thus this psychic point appears, disappears, reappears, redisappears, again reappears, becomes dim, disappears, reappears, again goes dimmer and dimmer. Ultimately what happens? It becomes absolutely black and becomes one with the psychic background.

This will practically take you 5 minutes as a beginner, but after good practice in *trataka* one single round (this is called one round) will take half an hour. Three minutes gaze and twenty-seven mutes visualization of the psychic point within appearing, disappearing, appearing, disappearing. This is one point. Those who will practise this will find another phenomenon. That is: the moment you close your eyes, the psychic dot appearing in *chidakasha* will go upward. And when it goes upward many aspirants will find it absolutely disturbing, because after a certain time they do not know where to look to. They cannot look up further, and the psychic dot goes up and up. Those who have practised *shambhavi-mudra*, they are able to steady that psychic point in *bindu chakra*. That *bindu* goes upward and tries to become one with this *chakra*.[13]

Then what is to be done? There is some way out. For beginners it should be like this: when they look at the candle flame for some time and close their eyes seeing the psychic dot moving upwards, they

[13] http://www.yogamag.net/archives/2005/cmar05/tratak.shtml

must follow it. When they cannot follow it any more they should lower their vision again and discover the point again. When they have discovered it, it again moves upwards. Again it will disappear and again they have to discover the point, until the point merges with the dark background. When in spite of one's best efforts, he is unable to locate it anymore, unable to discover it, he should open his eyes and do another round of *trataka.* So far as spiritual practice is concerned and for the sake of concentration and manifestation of the inner vision, one should close his eyes much before the strain takes place and tears roll down. A practitioner must be able to judge himself in such a way that if he closes his eyes, the eyes will not burn, tears will not roll down.

Do eleven rounds. It is said that eleven rounds of *trataka* make one *dharana*, which means mental conception becoming clear. When you think of a cow and you see a cow in your mind, it is called *dharana.* When you are only thinking of it and not seeing it, then it is called *kalpana* (imagination), a lower state of *kalpana. Dharana* is a higher state of *kalpana. Dharana* is imagination and clear-cut conception.

Gradually there should be the intensity of your psychic conception. When this state has arrived, meditation begins. Unless the object of meditation actually becomes clear, within the field of vision, there in no hope for anyone to get into meditation and much less hope to get into *samadhi.*

On Darkness

Sit alone in the dark and practise *trataka* on the darkness. The eyes should be open fully. Continue to see in the darkness without any light. Sit there daily and practise it steadily and firmly.

On Blue Sky

Sit in an open place or on the terrace at the end of the day and gaze at the blue sky without blinking. Try to feel that you have become like the sky or that the sky has come nearer to you. In due course the consciousness of the practitioner becomes so transformed that even though the object is in front of your eyes, you are not aware of it. The consciousness which separates the seer and the seen does not remain separate, but identifies with the object.

On Photograph

Have a small photograph of your chosen deity. Take a sheet of blank paper, the size of a book, and cut out a circle two inches in diameter, so that there is a round open space in the paper. Now place the photo of your deity behind the paper, fixing it in such a manner that you can only see the face through the hole, and frame it under glass. During the day practise *trataka* on the photo. The photo should be straight in front of the eyes at a distance of one and a half feet. Try not to take your vision outside the circle.

On Havana (Offering Oblations into the Flame of Fire)

Perform *havana* daily and in the sacrificial fire put scented objects. When the fire has ignited and has burned steadily for some time, repeat a prayer to the fire-god Jataveda and perform *trataka* on the flame. Try to think of the divine being in the flame while doing *trataka.*

On Crystal

If you happen to have a crystal, practise *trataka* on it. This is an independent and important *sadhana.* When you are practising *trataka* into a crystal you should look into the crystal as long as possible without winking your eyes. But the moment the eyes get tired close them and take rest. You do not have to think of the crystal when eyes are closed, you see nothing. There is a special rule for the crystal gazing: Though no tears should fall down, and your eyes should not be strained, gazing for about ten minutes are allowed.

On Shivalinga

Worship a *shivalinga* daily with great devotion. Concentrate on the water being poured on it. The *shivalinga* must be of a black stone. If it is a really black stone, make a sandalwood mark on it and steady your eyes on the mark. Otherwise try to concentrate on the entire black *linga*.

On Flower

Take a red, white or yellow flower. It should preferably be a dark coloured flower. If it is a red rose, keep it in the light and practise *trataka* on it. If it is a white or yellow flower, then practise in a dark room.

On Flower on Cloth

Take a black or a dark green cloth, 2 ft wide and 3 ft long. Hang it on the wall in front of you and in the centre of it pin a yellow, white or pink rose. Now sit in front of the flower in a semi-dark room and practise *trataka* on it.

On Metal Object

Take any small article made of bright metal, like vessels that shine when polished. It may be of brass, copper, silver or gold, for instance, an incense burner, a small jug or a *panchapatra*. It should be no more than two inches in height. Practise *trataka* on that bright object in half light.

On Your Shadow

In the morning, stand with your back to the sun and practise *trataka* on the shadow of your neck.

On Moon

Practise *trataka* on the full moon or when the moon rises at night.

On Water

Sit down on a riverbank or raised ground where you can see the current of water for a long distance. Practise *trataka* on the water. The eyes should remain steadily fixed on one spot; they should not move along the waves.

On Changing Scenes

While you are travelling in a train, open the window, keep the eyes open and watch distant scenes, without any emotion at all. The eyelids should not flicker, in spite of the changing scenes. The eyeballs should be completely steady and the mind devoid of any feeling. Thus you can also do spiritual practices while travelling.

On Needle

Keep a needle hanging on the wall and practise *trataka* on it. At the time of performing *trataka*, ensure that no other object is visible and that no other thought comes to the mind.

On Idol

Take an idol roughly 3 to 4 inches high and put it at some distance. Fix your eye on the idol and start developing concentration. If you do not have an idol, take a picture instead. Make sure that the picture is not coloured.

With the idol or picture before, you start fixing your gaze on the eye of the idol or picture as the case may be. You must concentrate your gaze at the pointed object without least deviation or disturbance. It must be a one-point gaze. You should not deflect your eye unless you feel your own eye watering. By practice, this technique can be acquired automatically. At this stage you better take rest for some time. After taking sufficient rest you should close your eyes and bring forth the idol or picture in your vivid imagination and then put it to *trataka* practice. At least 20 or 25 times you should bring forth the idol or picture into your imagination.

After a regular practice spread over a few days the practitioner will be able to bring forth in his imagination the idol or picture without slightest delay. Initially the idol will remain in his concrete imagination no more than a minute or so. Gradually the practitioner will find the idol staying in his imagination for a longer duration.

In the beginning your mind's eye or visual imagination will see many things in addition to the idol or picture. Gradually it will settle down to a one-point concentration on the specific target. Again, this concentration will give the practitioner the power to see any event or thing or person, should he desire to see.

In order to see this desired object the practitioner should bring *trataka* to bear on such objects, in addition to the idol or picture. He should try to visualize them as long as possible.

This practice paves the way for the opening of the third eye. As one closes one's eyes and brings *trataka* to bear on the idol placed before, the process of the opening of the third eye begins to assume shape. By this practice the ganglion supporting the third eye gets strengthened.

PRECAUTIONS AND SUGGESTIONS

1. Eyes should be splashed and washed with cold water immediately after the *trataka* practice. This will stimulate the blood supply in the eye regions.
2. Avoid using external eye medicine or solution after *trataka*. Also avoid rubbing the eyes, even if in the beginning of *trataka* you feel some eye strain, which would be due to adaptation to eye exercises.
3. Avoid doing *trataka* on the burning sun. For better eye health, it is advised to sit with closed eyes, facing the sun. *Trataka* on the sun with open eyes should be performed in the early morning and late afternoon (i.e. sunset). However, *trataka* on the full moon of *purnamasi* is the best.
4. Some bodily exercises before and after *trataka* are necessary to revitalize the tissues and nerves.
5. The continuous repetition and reflection upon the symbol of Ishvara, i.e. *aum*, during *trataka* practice will be very beneficial spiritually.
6. *Trataka* should definitely be practised for at least 5 minutes before beginning any *sadhana*. When one wants the mind to

be concentrated, *trataka* should be performed on any object for some time, or inner *trataka* may be practised. Students especially should practise *trataka*. Its daily practice will help them to develop concentration and memory power as well as improve their eyesight.

7. When should you practise *trataka*? Crystal gazing in dim light. Gazing at a dot in bright light. Gazing at a candle at any time.
8. *Trataka* can be done at any time but is more effective when performed on an empty stomach. The most suitable time is between 4 and 6 in the morning after *asana* and *pranayama* practice.
9. If you wish to delve deeper into the mind, *trataka* should be done late at night before going to bed and before *japa* (meditation).
10. During the practice of *trataka* the breathing must be slow, rhythmic and deep. This will bring steadiness to the breathing process, making the body and mind steady also. One can always control the onslaught of desire or anger by practising the elementary stage of *trataka* when excited. When any emotional shock is experienced, the practice of *trataka* is as beneficial as the practice of *kumbhaka*. *Trataka* opens up a storehouse of energy.

ADVANTAGES

Trataka eradicates all eye diseases, fatigue and sloth and closes the doorway creating these problems. *Trataka* benefits not only the eyes but a whole range of physiological and mental functions. It is therapeutic in depression, insomnia, allergy, anxiety, postural problems, poor concentration and memory.

Trataka unlocks the inherent energy of the mind and channelizes it to the dormant areas of the unconscious. Yogi Swatmarama mentions the arousal of clairvoyance but other capabilities such as telepathy, telekinesis and psychic healing can also develop. Not only that, further results of one-pointedness of mind are strong will-power, improved memory and concentrative ability. Physiologically, *trataka* relieves eye ailments such as eye strain and headache, myopia, astigmatism and even early stages of cataract. The eyes become clear bright, able to see the reality beyond appearances.

The mind becomes very steady while performing *trataka* and when it is concentrated, a person sees visions. This is called the vision of the divine being. So long as one remains awake, the mental tendencies become involved in many external objects, but at the time of sleep they turn inwards and become centrifugal. In this stage people dream, these dreams being the formations of their past impressions. During the practice of *trataka* the mind becomes concentrated and the aspirant begins to see dreams which correspond to the predominant thought or mental attitude.

For simplification, we have named that power of thought and knowledge through which the senses function as the mind. It is because of the mind that we are absorbed in the world. The mind has been said to be the cause of the bondage of the soul, and also of the experiences of happiness and misery. It should also be remembered that the mind is an instrument of self-elevation, the inspirer of emancipation. When the tendencies of the mind flow towards sources of enjoyment, it becomes the cause of our downfall and unhappiness. When the mind flies towards higher objects, it becomes the instrument for achieving efficiency in action and for developing intelligence, knowledge and liberation.

We are not concerned here with whether the mind is biological or psychological, but with the fact that it constitutes a medium for working in this world. It is also the instrument for acquiring knowledge and virtue, and also for the realization of God and the soul.

The impression of the object falls on the optic nerves. The shadow of the object falls on the eyes and then on the retina. The optic nerves of the retina are connected by the sensory nerves with the brain. The brain has several centres which are connected with the optic nerves. These centres receive information through the optic nerves and send out commands. Many of these centres are asleep or inactive. *Trataka* does not merely increase the function of perception. Through the medium of perception, the centres of the brain which remain inactive in an ordinary person are awakened. Man is capable of becoming a superman if he is able to awaken and activate those glands and nerve centres which in the natural course of evolution are in an inactive state.

The dreams follow the mental patterns of the aspirant and reveal themselves as a reality or as symbols. A tamasic *sadhaka* has perverse dreams which indicate a different meaning. A rajasic *sadhaka* sees symbolic dreams, while a sattvic aspirant sees true visions. This is possible only when there is intensified awareness and concentrated consciousness.

Trataka makes the mind steady and helps it to concentrate. Therefore, when an individual does any intellectual work, listens carefully to something or thinks about something, the eyes remain steady without a flicker, and thus a natural state of *trataka* is attained. This faculty can be applied consciously whenever necessary.

Pain can be eliminated through *trataka*. Many diseases and afflictions are also cured. The poison of a scorpion bite can be eliminated by *trataka* on the affected area. In the same way *trataka* can be performed on a diseased part of the body. In this case, the eyes become the medium for the transmission of healing power.

The first step on the path of spirituality is to control the mind and make it useful. The first *sadhana* of a *sadhaka* consists of understanding the mind, in knowing its direction and turning it upwards. The *sadhana* of *trataka* will help you a great deal in understanding the mind and making its unseen powers active, so as to prepare you for self-realization.

The practice of *trataka* is independent in its own way and is meant for aspirants of higher categories. *Trataka* is a very powerful *sadhana*. Gandhari had mastered *trataka*. Ramana Maharshi also practised *trataka*. Many *sadhus* in the mountains have practised this *sadhana*. *Trataka* shows us that the eyes are the instruments by which the mind and the soul are reached.

DIFFICULTIES IN TRATAKA

There are certain difficulties which are encountered in the practice of *trataka*. It is difficult to keep the eyes steady because drooping of the eyelids is a natural tendency and it is difficult to keep them from drooping, even with effort, for a long time. It is also difficult to gaze steadily at one central point continuously in the beginning.

Another difficulty is that the eyes water every now and then. Those who are not used to sitting in one posture for a long time encounter further difficulties. Continuous gazing at one object makes the object appear as if it is two. Sometimes the black dot appears white and vice versa. Finally, the *sadhaka* is often overcome by uncontrollable sleep during the practice of *trataka*.

A *sadhaka* has to overcome these difficulties, but it is not difficult if one is alert and firmly fixed on one's ideal. For people of firm determination, the difficulties are surmountable. The practice should be increased gradually and slowly. A concentrated mind is a great help to an aspirant. Everything becomes easy for one who practices with devotion, steadiness and sincerity.

Now you can practise this *sadhana* yourself. Select any of the above-mentioned methods of *trataka*, according to your choice. By regular practice you will achieve knowledge of *yoga* through your own experience. There is nothing higher than self-experience and there is no joy greater than practising *sadhana*.[14]

Meditation

By the definite science of meditation known for millenniums to

[14] http://thedivinepowerwithinyou.blogspot.in/2013/07/the-wonders-of-tratak html

> the *yogis* and sages of India, and to Jesus, any seeker of God can enlarge the calibre of his consciousness to omniscience to receive within himself the Universal Intelligence of God.
>
> – Paramahansa Yogananda

Meditation (*dhyana*) is the seventh step in *raja-yoga* of Maharshi Patanjali. Meditation is not a part of any religion; it is a science. In meditation, the mind is clear, relaxed and inwardly focused. When you meditate, you are fully awake and alert, but your mind is not focused on the external world or on the events taking place around you. Meditation requires an inner state that is still and one-pointed so that the mind becomes silent. When the mind is silent and no longer distracts you, meditation deepens.

From childhood onward, we have been educated only to examine and verify things in the external world. No one has taught us how to look within, to find within and to verify within. Therefore, we remain strangers to ourselves, while trying to get to know others. This lack of self-understanding is one of the main reasons our relationships don't seem to work, and why confusion and disappointment so often prevail in our life. Except for the practice of meditation, there is no method to truly develop control over the totality of the mind.

The goal of meditation is to go beyond the mind and experience our essential nature — which is described as peace, happiness and bliss. But as anyone who has tried to meditate knows, the mind itself is the biggest obstacle standing between us and this awareness. The mind is undisciplined and unruly, and it resists any attempt to discipline it or to guide it on a particular path. The mind has a mind of its own. That is why many people sit for meditation and experience only fantasies, daydreams or hallucinations. We are taught how to move and behave in the outer world, but we are never taught how to be still and examine what is within ourselves. When we learn to do this through meditation, we attain the highest of all joys that can ever be experienced by a human being. All the other joys in the world are momentary, but the joy of meditation is immense and everlasting. This is not an exaggeration; it is a truth supported by a long line of sages, both those who renounced the world and attained truth, and those who continued living in the world yet remained unaffected by it.

Learning how to be still is the method of meditation. The process of cultivating stillness begins with the body. In the *yoga* tradition, you are guided by a competent teacher to keep your head, neck and trunk straight while sitting in a meditative posture (*asana*). When you have learned to be comfortable in this posture, you should form a regular habit of practising in the same postures.

Have patience and do your practice systematically. Every action has a reaction. It is not possible for you to meditate and not receive benefits. You may not notice those benefits now, but slowly and gradually you are storing the *samskaras* (impressions) in the unconscious mind that will help you later. If you sow a seed today, you don't reap the fruit tomorrow, but eventually you will. It takes time to see results; be gentle with yourself.[15]

Meditation has been laid stress upon by all religions. The meditative state of mind is declared by the *yogis* to be the highest state in which the mind exists. When the mind is studying the external object, it gets identified with it, loses itself. To use the simile of the old Indian philosopher: the soul of man is like a piece of crystal, but it takes the colour of whatever is near it. Whatever the soul touches . . . it has to take its colour. That is the difficulty. That constitutes the bondage. The colour is so strong, the crystal forgets itself and identifies itself with the colour. Suppose a red flower is near the crystal and the crystal takes the colour and forgets itself, thinks it is red. We have taken the colour of the body and have forgotten what we are. All the difficulties that follow come from that one dead body. All our fears, all worries, anxieties, troubles, mistakes, weakness, evil, are front that one great blunder — that

[15] Swami Vivekananda's lecture, delivered at the Washington Hall, San Francisco, 3 April 1900.

we are bodies. This is the ordinary person. It is the person taking the colour of the flower near to it. We are no more bodies than the crystal is the red flower. The practice of meditation is pursued. The crystal knows what it is, takes its own colour. It is meditation that brings us nearer to truth than anything else.[16]

Swami Vivekananda would regularly practise meditation. Once "After about one and a half hour, Swamiji rose from meditation with the words 'Shiva, Shiva' ". His eyes were flushed, the expression placid, calm and grave. Bowing before Sri Ramakrishna he came downstairs and paced the courtyard of the Math. After a while he said to the disciple. "Do you see how the *sadhus* are practising meditation, etc. nowadays?"

Once Vivekananda said:

> When the meditation is deep, one sees many wonderful things. While meditating at the Baranagore Math, one day I saw the nerves *ida* and *pingala*. One can see them with a little effort. Then, when one has a vision of the *sushumna*, one can see anything one likes. If a man has unflinching devotion to the *guru*, spiritual practices — meditation, *japa*, and so forth — come quite naturally; one need not struggle for them. The *guru* is Brahma, the *guru* is Vishnu, and the *guru* is Shiva Himself.
>
> Within there is the lion — the eternally pure, illumined, and ever free *atman*; and directly one realizes Him through meditation and concentration, this world of *maya* vanishes.

The rise of these waves, or thoughts, during meditation is an evidence that your mind is tending towards concentration. Sometimes the mind is concentrated on a set of ideas — this is called meditation with *vikalpa* (oscillation). But when the mind becomes almost free from all activities, it melts in the inner Self, which is the essence of infinite knowledge, One, and itself its own support. This is what is called *nirvikalpa samadhi*, free from all activities.

A meditating mind is like an unwavering flame. It's a state of

---

[16] http://www.vivekananda.net/Lectures Meditation.html

an inner absorption. To get absorbed in the inner self, we say, "I am beautiful or I am miserable or I am educated . . ." but who is this I? This is a profound question. In meditation we try to come nearer to our divine core. In meditation we try to imagine our divinity. Once a man asked Swami Vivekananda: "Are you trying to hypnotize us by telling us to imagine divinity within us?" Swamiji answered: "You are already hypnotized by your body and mind; I am trying to dehypnotize you." In meditation we try to concentrate on our own divinity in the form of God. During meditation try not to get caught by the thoughts of self-achievements or suffering that you underwent in the world.

Try to have a practical routine of meditation. It's better to meditate early in the morning. If you are hungry then have a light snacks before meditation. Initially mind may not like the alien practice but if you persevere for some days then you will find peace.

Meditation can be practised at any place but places with spiritual vibrations are more conducive. Occasionally keep flowers in your room. Flowers have got a tendency to elevate the mind. In your room do not think of any negative or harmful thoughts. A holy atmosphere will automatically get created inside your own room. If mind is holy then the room becomes holy.

Many different types of meditations are there. There are many ways of meditation. Choose one — whichever suits you, whichever you like. Not that you do one today and another tomorrow and another, the day after and another, the other day. No. Take one and finish it and just stick on to it. Go with it. All the ways are good, but take one way and go deep into it.

To begin with only meditate for 15 minutes each day. If you spend long time everyday in initial stage then mind will start find excuses for stopping the practice.

ADVANTAGES

Daily meditation practice brings peace of mind, inner joy and inner peace. By increasingly gaining control over your mind, every session brings you closer and closer to your own Self, the centre of your being filled with joy, wisdom and bliss.

Meditation helps you understand how your mind works, and when you understand how your mind works you can begin to make purposeful changes to your life to improve it. Additionally, meditation improves your ability to objectively analyse your emotions, mental states, thought patterns and responses to events that occur around you.

Regular meditation opens the avenues of intuitive knowledge, makes the mind calm and steady, awakens an ecstatic feeling and brings the yogic students in contact with the source of the Supreme *Purusha* (God). If there are doubts, they are all cleared by themselves when you march on the path of *dhyana-yoga* steadily.

When you meditate regularly your mind becomes clearer and more focused, thereby improving your quality of life and allowing you to perform better and more quickly all tasks you choose to be involved in. Not only can meditation help you reach your goals quicker, but also and more importantly, it can guide you in setting better and wiser goals in life.

There are also numerous benefits for the physical body. Studies have shown that the regular practice of meditation can assist one in lowering blood pressure, decreasing stress, improving memory and bring in a host of other health benefits.

SOME IMPORTANT POINTS

1. Attachment to perishable worldly objects and relations cannot bring peace. One has to attach oneself to one's higher Self. Serve people by seeing the same Self in everyone.
2. The way to change others is to first change oneself.
3. If you want to concentrate the mind stop feeding it with negative and lower things and instead feed it with positive thoughts.

4. So long as you have desires, you cannot achieve complete stability of mind.
5. In a negative atmosphere it is very difficult to meditate but with preparation and practice it can be possible.
6. Having one central goal in life can lead to integration of personality. One should have an ideal along with our ambition. Self-realization should be the highest goal, other things should be subservient to that.
7. Strengthen your convictions by reading holy books.
8. Spiritual development is a slow process; it's a process of inner evolution. Regular spiritual practice has profound effect in the long run even if immediate effects are invisible.
9. Self-discipline with regard to food, sleeping hours, self-study and all other activities of life can help us strengthen our mental immune system.
10. After long practice of meditation duality disappears and *samadhi*, the superconscious state, is attained.

PREPARATION FOR THE PRACTICE

Choose an Ideal Time for Meditation

The *hours of sunrise and sunset*, while nature transitions between day and night, are ideal for the practice of meditation. Early morning: 4 to 6 a.m. is the best time for meditation when nature is calm, peaceful and more energetic. If anyway you miss the morning time, you practise in the evening or any time when you know you are not likely to be disturbed and are free to relax and enjoy.

Choose a Quiet Place

Just like a convenient hour, choose a place where you not likely to be disturbed. Quiet and peaceful surroundings can make the meditation experience more *enjoyable and relaxing*. Although the natural places like the hills, mountains, bank of the rivers and seas, gardens, etc. are considered appropriate as they are full of natural beauty and free from noise and pollution. Even holy places like temples are considered suitable for meditation as they are already charged with spiritual energy which helps the aspirant enter the depth of meditation. Even neat and clean and lone places in your own home are suitable for meditation practice.

Sit in a Comfortable Posture

Your posture makes a difference too. You can sit in any meditative postures like *sukhasana*, *siddhasana*, *padmasana*, *svastikasana* in which you are relaxed, comfortable and steady. Sit straight with your spine erect; keep your shoulders and neck relaxed, and eyes closed throughout the process.

Keep a Relatively Empty Stomach

A good time to meditate at home — or in office — is *before having a meal.* After food, you might doze off while meditating. However, do not force yourself to meditate when you are very hungry. You will find it difficult because of hunger cramps or you may even keep thinking about food the whole time. In this case, you can meditate after two hours after having food.

Start With a Few Warm-ups

A few warm-up or *sukshma yoga* exercises before sitting to meditate helps improve circulation, removes inertia and restlessness and makes the body feel lighter.

Take a Few Deep Breaths

This is again preparation for easy meditation. Deep breathing in and out as well as doing some *pranayamas* like *anuloma-viloma* and *bhramari* before meditating are always considered good. This helps to steady the rhythm of the breath and leads the mind into a peaceful meditative state.

Be Calm and Peaceful

Be calm and peaceful. There should be no facial stress or strain. A gentle smile throughout keeps you relaxed, peaceful and enhances your *meditation experience*. Eyes should be gently closed.

Open Your Eyes Slowly and Gently

As you come close to the end of the meditation, don't be in a hurry to open your eyes and start moving about. *Open your eyes slowly* and gradually and take time to become aware of yourself and your surroundings.

SOME MEDITATION PRACTICES

Experiment with whatever technique appeals to you. And remember, not all techniques suit everyone; what suits you may not suit your friend. And having practised a method for some months, you may find you have outgrown it. There is nothing sacrosanct about meditative methods: they are practical means to access a natural, inherent quality. Feel free to playfully experiment with them.

Having selected the method, try it for at least seven days consecutively. And when you are trying it out, give it all you have got. By then you will know whether the initial attraction has been confirmed or not. If you feel that this is your method, make a commitment to continue it for a minimum of three months. After three months you can continue with it or choose another.

Continuity is important. It's like heating water: up to 99^0 it is still water and if you stop there it will cool down and you will have to reheat it. But if you persevere to 100^0, then the water takes a quantum leap and is transformed into vapour.

A Simple Breathing Meditation

The first stage of meditation is to stop distracting thoughts and make our mind clearer and more lucid. This can be achieved by practising a simple breathing meditation.

We choose a quiet place to meditate and then sit in a comfortable position. We can sit in the traditional cross-legged posture or in any other position that is comfortable. If we wish, we can sit in a chair.

It is important to keep our back straight to prevent our mind from becoming sluggish or sleepy.

We sit with our eyes partially closed and turn our attention to our breathing. We try to breathe naturally, preferably through the nostrils, without attempting to control our breath, and become aware of the sensation of the breath as it enters and leaves the nostrils.

This sensation is our object of meditation. We should try to concentrate on it to the exclusion of anything else.

To start with, our mind will be very busy, and it might even seem that the meditation is making our mind busier; but in reality we are just starting to notice how busy our mind actually is.

There will be a great temptation to follow the different thoughts as they arise, but we should resist this and remain focused single-pointedly on the sensation of the breath.

If we notice that our mind has wandered and is following our thoughts, we should immediately return it to the breath. We should repeat this as many times as necessary until the mind settles on the breath.

Meditation on Being a Seer and Witness

- Sit comfortably in any meditative posture with spinal cord straight.
- Do normal breathing. Gently close your eyes.
- Ask yourself what, "what am I thinking"?
- See your thoughts, do not stop your thoughts, do not suppress any thoughts, let a thought come and watch it.
- Make a special effort to find out what you are thinking.
- Ask yourself, "What am I thinking now"?
- Watch every thought, do not become a thinker but become a seer.
- Do not lose yourself in the thoughts, but remain detached from the thinking process.

- Do not identify yourself with your thoughts but remain an impartial spectator of your thoughts.
- Do not like or dislike a thought. Do not love or hate a thought, do not run after it, let it come.
- You just see it, as you are only a seer.
- Whether thoughts are of pain or pleasure, see them impartially like a seer and as an impartial spectator.
- Expose each and every thought before your consciousness.
- If there is no thought, then be aware of that. When there is anxiety, then see it.
- If there is restlessness, try to be a spectator.
- If there is peace, see it.
- Do not identify yourself with piece and anxiety and with pain and pleasure.
- Be aloof, and say I am not the thinker; I am the seer of my thoughts.
- "I am not a hearer"; "I am the seer of the hearing".
- If you hear any disturbing sound from the surrounding, do not react but witness it.
- Concentrate on every item of thought and thus overcome it.
- Now you see and hear everything in this universe as a seer and an impartial spectator.
- Just see and witness whatever is happening in this whole universe as a seer.
- Practise this for 15 to 30 minutes.
- Gently open your eyes and see the world and the whole universe as a seer for a few seconds.

Meditation on the Rising Sun

The "Sun Meditation" is very simple but very soothing, recharging and effective. It energizes the whole body and calms the mind. This meditation is done in the morning when the sun is rising. But if you have missed the rising sun you meditate on the rising sun through your imagination whenever you have the time. Enjoy the full glory of the sun and experience deeper meditation.

- Sit comfortably in any meditative and comfortable pose.
- If you are practising early in the morning at the dawn when the sun is rising you look at the rising sun for 3 to 5 minutes.
- Now gently close your eyes. Feel the sun's rays falling on you, on your forehead.
- Now allow your body to soak in the sunlight. Feel the sun's rays illuminating every cell of your body.
- Envision the interior of your body aglow in red light as the blood pulses with sunlight through your veins.
- Now visualize the organs: head, skull, heart, lungs, kidney, liver, chest, back, hands, legs, eyes, etc. are glowing with sunlight. Every organs and cells are lit with fiery light. Know that inside your body every part of you is aware of the sun.
- Now your whole body is filled with golden light that is radiating from the images of the sun.
- Don't think anything. Just imagine and feel the light extend all around you to 3 ft front of the body, side of the body and back of the body. Feel that you are surrounded by sunlight.
- Now you are fully immersed into the sun rays. Take it deeply and feel its nourishment.
- Your eyes are still closed, just mentally spread your awareness and feel the light extending into the whole room or the place where you are sitting.
- Now slowly open your eyes. Rub your hands, make them slightly warm and keep it on your face and now start your day. Now you are physically, mentally and spiritually fully recharged. You are full of divine potentials and dynamic energy. Your birth and life have some great goal and purpose which you could achieve as all the great persons of the globe have done so far. Now you are one of them, ready to convert impossible into possible.

At Night

- Even while lying on the bed at night you can practise this meditation.
- Lie down on the bed and relax for a few minutes, after few minutes when you find yourself moving into your sleep, then repeat the above process.
- If you fall asleep doing this, it is perfectly alright. Your subconscious mind will continue and finish the meditation anyway.
- Then people around you will start noticing a glow or some kind of radiance.

Meditation on the Full Moon Light

Full moon meditation is a great way to harness the power of nature in order to heal your own mind, body and soul. The moon is a symbol of piousness and coolness. Therefore the full moon meditation naturally brings piousness and coolness within the aspirant. The full moon is a time of positive opportunity if you use it correctly. It can increase your positive energy and purify your emotions. Since the full moon pours down so much energy, meditating during this time creates calm, mindfulness and stillness. The night of the full moon is a special time, especially for those who are following a spiritual path that gives them a special connection to the moon. People may celebrate the full moon in any number of ways, such as choosing to spend some time out in the fresh night air enjoying its light. One of the most popular ways that people choose to celebrate the time of the full moon, however, is with intensive and cleansing meditation.

There are many reasons to choose to meditate at the time of the full moon. Many individuals may find themselves to be unusually agitated or emotional at this point in the month. That is not surprising, as the moon is deeply and intimately connected with our mind and our thoughts. Meditation can help to cleanse these feelings of agitation and can even provide us with a great opportunity to let go of the mental or emotional baggage that has been weighing us down. Meditating at the full moon can also help us to unleash our creativity, whether we are focused on specific creative endeavours or are simply in need of a new way of thinking about the problems and issues we are facing in our day-to-day lives. This can be practised indoor and outdoor.

If you meditate indoors, determine whether there is a location in your home that will let you see the moon. Clear out a space where you can sit comfortably in the light. This can help you to get the most out of this meditative practice. Consider the use of a *mantra*, if that will help you focus. The amount of time that you meditate will depend on your ability to keep your mind clear and your patience with the task. The longer you are able to meditate the better.

- Sit in any comfortable posture with spine erect.
- Wear comfortable clothing, and be sure that the space where you are seated is comfortable as well. If you are outside, think about using a blanket, so no items or objects, or even insects, disturb you.
- Clear your mind. Focus your attention on the light of the moon and nothing else.
- Release all of the anxiety, tension and stress that have been bothering you and allow your mind to empty completely. Remember not to become frustrated if stray thoughts creep in. Simply release them as they occur and return to your meditative state.
- Continue breathing in the pure white light energy of the full moon, drinking the moonbeams of love into your very soul.
- Getting a sense now of every cell in your body being cleansed and purified.
- With your inner sight you may even be able to see your organs, such as your liver, being energized, purified and filled with transformational white light.
- Feeling or seeing your energy field expanding, as it is filling with white light, you are beginning to comfortably lose awareness of the boundary of your physical body.

- Now mix your mind with the moonbeams.
- Wash your sorrows in their rays. Feel the mystic light spreading silently over your body, over trees, over vast lands, standing in an open space with quiet eyes.
- Behold beyond the limits of the moonbeam-revealed scenery, the bedimmed fringe of the shining horizon.
- Let your meditation run past the rim of the visible to the lands of fancy.
- Spread your mind from the moonbeam – visible objects to the dim stars and distant skies lying beyond in the eternal stillness of the ether, all throbbing with life.
- Watch the moonbeams spread, not only on one side of the earth, but everywhere in the eternal region of your spacious mind.
- Meditate until, in the cool moonbeams of your calmness, you race over trackless skies and in realization, behold the universe as light.
- Now relax and gently open your eyes.

Meditation on Who Am I?

Meditate that I am the omnipresent *atman*. "I am neither the body, nor the mind, nor the *buddhi* (determining faculty), neither the gross nor the subtle body."

By this process of elimination, immerse your mind in the transcendent knowledge which is your real nature. Kill the mind by thus plunging it repeatedly in this.

You realize and are established in your real nature.

This "I" personality does not exist now. And meditating upon this as infinite eternal being. I have now entered into a consciousness of non-dual, pure identity with the Supreme Being.

I am infinite. I am spaceless. I am tireless. I am beyond body, thought and utterance, I am beyond all matter and mind. I am endless bliss.

I and Thou art the same: *aham brahma asmi, so 'ham, sivo 'ham, tat tvam asi, ayamatma brahma, sacchidanando 'ham.*

I am Truth, Bliss and Consciousness.

Meditation on God's Light

- Sit comfortably in any comfortable *asana* with spine erect.
- Do deep inhalation and exhalation.
- Be physically and mentally relaxed.
- Look at a light and gently close your eyes.
- Forget the darkness around you and watch the bright red colour within your eyelids.
- Look intently into that violet-red colour.
- Meditate on it and imagine that it is becoming bigger and bigger.
- Behold around you a dimly shining sea of violet light.
- You are a wave of light, a ripple of peace floating on the surface of the sea.
- Now watch carefully. You, the little wave, are tossing on an ocean of light.
- Your tiny life is a part of the all-pervading life.
- As your meditation deepens, you, a little shallow wave of peace, are becoming the deep, wide ocean of peace.
- Meditate on the thought, "I am a wave of peace".
- Feel the vastness just beneath your consciousness. The wave should feel the sustaining life of the vast ocean beneath it.
- Behind the wave of my consciousness is the sea of cosmic consciousness.
- And is the supporting ocean of Thy vastness.
- Thy light of peace, power and purity is ever shining through me.
- Now gently open your eyes and be relaxed.

Meditation on the Cosmic Sound

- Sit comfortably in any comfortable *asana* with spine erect.

- Do deep inhalation and exhalation.
- Be physically and mentally relaxed.
- Now listen to the cosmic sound of *aum*, a great *hum* of countless atoms in the sensitive right side of your head.
- This is the voice of God. Feel the sound spreading through the brain. Hear its continuous pounding roar.
- Now hear and feel its surging into the spine, bursting open the doors of the heart.
- Feel it resounding through every tissue, every feeling and every cord of your nerves.
- Every blood cell, every thought is dancing on the sea of roaring vibration.
- Observe the spreading volume of the cosmic sound. It sweeps through the body and mind into the earth and the surrounding atmosphere. You are moving with it, into the airless ether and into millions of universes of matter.
- Meditate on the marching spread of the cosmic sound. It has passed through the physical universes to the subtle shining veins of rays that hold all matter in manifestation.
- The cosmic sound is commingling with millions of multicoloured rays. The cosmic sound has entered the realm of cosmic rays.
- Listen to, behold, and feel the embrace of the cosmic sound and the eternal light.
- The cosmic sound now pierces through the heart fires of cosmic energy and they both melt within the ocean of cosmic consciousness and cosmic joy.
- The body melts into the universe. The universe melts into the soundless voice. The sound melts into the all-shining light.
- And the light enters the bosom of infinite joy.
- Now gently open your eyes and be relaxed.

Meditation on Enlightened Soul

- Sit comfortably in any comfortable *asana* with spine erect.

- Do deep inhalation and exhalation.
- Be physically and mentally relaxed.
- Gently close your eyes.
- Meditate that there is a sky within your heart.
- And within that sky manifests a light like the peak of the flame of fire.
- Meditate on this flame of fire as your soul.
- And again imagine an enlightened sky within the light of the flame of fire.
- That is the soul of your soul, the supreme soul that is God.

Meditation on Descending of Light

This is a specific method of meditation. Evening hours are considered the best time for the practice of meditation. This can be practised even while lying on bed or sitting in the arm chair.

- Sit comfortably in any comfortable *asana* with spine erect.
- Do deep inhalation and exhalation.
- Be physically and mentally relaxed.
- Gently close your eyes.
- Imagine and visualize that a stream of light has descended from the sky, from the sun-god.
- There is nothing but the beam of light spread all around you.
- Now this aura of light is entering your physical body through the navel region.
- All the internal organs, i.e. heart, lungs, kidney, lever, blood, bones, eyes, ears, hands, feets have got enlightened and radiating the beam of light.
- Second, meditate that within the brain are hidden innumerable centres of mental powers and thoughts.
- The steam of light has again descended and now it is entering the subtle body through the eyebrows centre, the *ajna chakra*.
- Now each and every brain cell is getting enlightened with that divine light.
- Now all the negative feelings, emotions have been wiped out

due to the touch of this light.

- Third, meditate on the heart region which is the seat of the causal body. This is also the dwelling place of the soul as the seers have visualized this through their yogic powers.
- Now imagine that the stream of light having descended from the sky is now entering the causal body and the dwelling place of the soul through the heart region, the *anahata chakra.*
- The stream of light is entering the small light of the soul which has now superbly got enlightened with its/this supreme light. This is just the communion of the individual soul with the universal or supreme soul. The individual consciousness and the universal/cosmic, supreme consciousness are now embracing each other.
- The individual soul is discarding and offering its narrowness and meanness to the universal soul, the Almighty God. On the other hand, the universal soul is offering its greatness to the individual soul. The small light of the individual soul is embracing the supreme light of God. Now with this communion the individual soul is experiencing the limitless, endless bliss.
- A great ocean of light has now manifested within the heart region. Feel how the great beam and current of light is passing through that limitless ocean. Many lotus flowers have blossomed in that ocean. This ocean is full of love, purity, compassion. Within the heart there is also a limitless sky. Numerous stars are twinkling in this limitless, endless sky. Just imagine and feel it.

Yoga-Nidra

Yoga-nidra is a "sleepless sleep". *Yoga-nidra* means psychic sleep. Sleep rests the body, but *yoga-nidra* rests both the mind and body. When you are asleep, your consciousness sleeps in your astral body, but in *yoga-nidra* your consciousness is awake within. *Yoga-nidra* performs two beneficial functions. It removes fatigue and invigorates the body. The stresses and strains of daily life create tensions and these rob the mind of its serenity. *Yoga-nidra* removes tensions and restores the elasticity of your mind.The evils of day-to-day life are deposited in our subconscious mind and in due course they exert a deleterious influence on our mental make-up. Just as our house must be swept daily to keep it tidy, to have a normal personality, we must remove the *samskaras*, the mental dirt.

Yoga-nidra is a state in which you are neither asleep nor awake. If you fall asleep, it is not *yoga-nidra*. If you remain awake, then too it is not *yoga-nidra*. If dreams overtake you, it is not *yoga-nidra*. *Yoga-nidra* is a state in which there is awareness of the conscious, subconscious and unconscious fields of your mind all at one time. It is a perfect therapy. It removes all psychological abnormalities and *samskaras*, and helps you to become your normal, natural self.

Patanjali has defined *yoga* as the controller of the *chitta vrittis* (mental modifications). Good behaviour is the outcome of the *chitta vrittis*; similarly, bad behaviour is also the outcome of the *chitta vrittis*. Our conscious, subconscious and unconscious fields are our *chitta*. Simultaneous awareness of these three fields is *aham asmi* (I am). This state in which you are aware but not aware that you are aware comes in *yoga-nidra*. Thereafter a process of sure but imperceptible sublimation takes place within.

It is said that meditation creates a fire which burns away our sins. What is sin? Actions which create uneasiness and abnormal feelings in the mind are sins. Cynics dismiss the word sin with a smile of derision. Whenever your conscience pricks you for any of your actions, that action is sin. Cynics are no exception to this rule; sin is there whether they admit it or not. In meditation your consciousness penetrates the various layers of your inner self. This is the fire that burns away the dross of *samskaras* within. Thereafter comes the yogic state of supreme peace and tranquillity of mind described in the second chapter of *Bhagavadgita*.

Yoga-nidra is one of the main techniques for the attainment of this peace. The all important point in *yoga-nidra* as well as in other meditation practices is that you must not allow yourself to fall asleep. In *yoga-nidra*, sleep tries to overpower you. If you can overcome this weakness, you will gain in willpower, and through willpower you can do great things in your life. If sleep comes, concentrate on the body or on the sleep itself as if it is trying to possess you and you are watching it. If images arise before your mind, go on watching them. In *yoga-nidra*, when you feel that you are unconscious, it actually means that you are conscious of being unconscious.

Yoga-nidra means yogic sleep. It is a state of conscious deep sleep. In meditation, you remain in the waking state of consciousness and gently focus the mind, while allowing thought patterns, emotions, sensations and images to arise and go on. However, in *yoga-nidra*, you leave the waking state, go *past* the dreaming state and go to deep sleep, yet remain awake. While *yoga-nidra* is a state that is very relaxing, it is also used by *yogi*s to purify the *samskara*s, the deep impressions that are the driving force behind *karma*. *Yoga-nidra* is not about "conscious effort" but "conscious relaxation". For example, the moment you hear the word "apple", its image instantly flashes through your mind. You don't need to put in an effort to think whether it's small or big, red or green. The same happens during *yoga-nidra*.

In meditation, you remain in the waking state of consciousness and gradually allow the layers of the unconscious and subconscious to come forward, expanding the waking state with one-pointed concentration and non-attachment to the streams of impressions flowing in the field of mind.

In *yoga-nidra*, you leave the waking state of consciousness, and go to the deep sleep state of consciousness, yet, paradoxically, remain fully awake. It is an extremely relaxing state in which *samskaras* of attachment and aversion, the driving force behind *karma*, are attenuated in strength.

Yoga-nidra can open latent potentiality of the mind. Its regular practice can relieve one from stress, frustrations, insomnia and psychosomatic diseases which have become a part of modern man's life. Most of the mental disturbances and psychosomatic diseases that people have these days are secondary to the fact that their mind is not stable, not balanced and they don't know how to access the immense potentiality of their mind. *Yoga-nidra* offers an opportunity to understand the mind and cut through its blind conditionings. It means sleeping with a trace of awareness. It is a kind of deep sleep in which you don't lose consciousness. Normally, people carry their frustrations, conflict, pain and turmoil with them when they go to sleep, and hence their sleep never goes deep. And due of this there remains great tension in their mind and body. The practice of *yoga-nidra* not only relaxes but restructures and reforms whole personality from within. It burns away old *samskaras*, habits and tendencies, paving the way to be born anew. If you practise *yoga-nidra* persistently, then the very nature of your mind can be changed, diseases can be cured and your creative genius can be restored. It also results in releasing of all muscular, emotional and mental tensions. It is a very effective form of complete psychic and physiological rest and rejuvenation. In *yoga-nidra*, the most effective means of training the mind is found in *sankalpa*. The mind is completely relaxed with heightened receptivity and hence it is easy to introduce the resolve. Anything in life can fail you but not your *sankalpa*, your resolve. When conscious mind and body is in deep relaxation, at that time whatever *sankalpa* you will make, it will get fulfilled. The resolution you make at the beginning of the practice is like sowing a seed and the resolution at the end is like irrigating it.

PRACTICE OF YOGA-NIDRA

Preparation

- Get ready for *yoga-nidra*. Lie down in *shavasana* (dead man's pose).

- Make yourself as comfortable as possible. Keep your feet apart and let them flop little sideways, arms slightly away from the body with the palms of your hands upwards.
- Gently close your eyes. Remember that you are about to practise *yoga-nidra*, psychic sleep and that you have only to maintain awareness of hearing and feeling. The body sleeps but the mind remains awake. You must remain alert so that you do not sleep. Say to yourself mentally: I will not sleep, I will remain awake.
- Take a deep breath and as you breathe in feel coolness and calmness spreading throughout the body. As you breathe out, feel your scares and worries flowing out of you, dropping away.

Relaxation

Become aware of sounds in the distance. Become aware of the most distant sounds that you can hear. Let your sense of hearing operate like a radar beam . . . searching out distant sounds and following them for a few seconds. Move your attention from sound to sound . . . without attempting to identify the source. Gradually bring your attention to closer sounds . . . to sounds outside this building . . . and then to sounds inside the building. Now develop your awareness of this room. . . . Without opening your eyes visualize the four walls, the ceiling, the floor, your body lying on the floor . . . total awareness of your body lying in perfect stillness. Your body is lying on the floor . . . develop your awareness of all the physical meeting points between your body and the floor. Become aware of the natural breath. Become aware of the deep, natural, spontaneous breath. Keep on listening to the instruction, and know that you are breathing. The practice of *yoga-nidra* begins now . . . say mentally to yourself: I am going to practise *yoga-nidra*. I will not sleep.

Resolve

This is the time to make your resolve. Simple resolve. . . . State your resolve clearly with feeling and awareness three times.

Rotation of Consciousness

Rotate your consciousness through different parts of the body. The practice always begins with the right hand.

Right Side

Right-hand thumb, second finger, third finger, fourth finger, fifth finger, palm of the hand, back of the hand, wrist, lower arm, elbow, upper arm, shoulder, armpit, waist, hip, right thigh, knee, calf muscle, ankle, heel, sole, top of the foot, right big toe, second toe, third toe, fourth toe, fifth toe.

Left Side

Left-hand thumb, second finger, third finger, fourth finger, fifth finger, palm of the hand, back of the hand, wrist, lower arm, elbow, upper arm, shoulder, armpit, waist, hip, left thigh, knee, calf muscle, ankle, heel, sole, top of the foot, left big toe, second toe, third toe, fourth toe, fifth toe.

Back

Right shoulder, left shoulder, right shoulder blade, left shoulder blade, right buttock, left buttock, the spine, the whole of the back together.

Front

Top of the head, forehead, right eyebrow, left eyebrow, the eyebrow centre, right eyelid, left eyelid, right eye, left eye, right ear, left you will make, it will get fulfilled. The resolution you make at the ear, right cheek, left cheek, nose, tip of the nose, right nostril, left nostril, upper lip, lower lip, chin, jaw, throat, right collarbone, left collarbone, right chest, left chest, middle of the chest, navel, abdomen, lower abdomen.

Major Parts

Whole of the right leg, whole of the left leg, both legs together, whole of the right arm, whole of the left arm, both arms together, whole of the back, whole of the front, whole of the head . . . together . . . legs, arms, back, front, head together, the whole of the body together.

Body/Floor Awareness

Become aware of the body . . . and the space that is occupied by your body . . . body and space. Become aware of the whole body and the floor, the whole body in relation to the floor . . . and be aware of the meeting points of the body and the floor.

Breathing

Be completely aware of your breathing . . . natural inhalation and exhalation. Maintain your awareness and at the same time start counting your breaths backwards from 10 to 1. Such as I am breathing in 10; I am breathing out 9; and so on. Feel the rise and fall of your breath from navel to the throat. The breathing is slow and relaxed.

Visualization

Imagine yourself in a park in the the early morning. . . . The sun has not risen and the park is deserted, except for yourself. It is a beautiful park, calm and peaceful . . . walk across the springy grass . . . listen to the birds chirping and call as they welcome the new day. There are gardens of flowers, roses, yellow, pink, red, purple, smell their fragrance and see the early morning dewdrops on their petals. Now see the sun is rising. You are lying down on the soft, delicate grass and seeing the sun that is just rising. You are just taking a sun bath. Each pore of your body is grasping the sunrays. All your inner organs, every cell of the body have grasped the sunrays. Now you're feeling very fresh and energetic. Meditate on the rising sun for a while.

Finish

Become aware of your breathing, become aware of your natural breath, become aware of the breath through your nostrils. Externalize your attention. Develop awareness of your surroundings

. . . the floor you are lying on , the room you are in. . . . Start making movements and sit up and gently open your eyes. The practice of *yoga-nidra* is now complete.[17]

[17] Saraswati, 2003, *Yoga Nidra*, p. 102.

Bibliography

Alok, T.D.S., 2003, *Sanskritik Patrakarita*, Panchkula: Grantha Akadami.

Aurobindo, Sri, 2000, *A Practical Guide to Integral Yoga*, 3rd edn, Pondicherry: Aurobindo Ashram.

Balkrishna, Acharya, 2007, *Yoga in Synergy with Medical Science*, Haridwar: Divya Prakashan, Patanjali Yogapeeth.

———, 2007, *Souvenir*, published during International Conference on Yoga for Health and Social Transformation, Haridwar: Divya Prakashan, Patanjali Yogapeeth.

CWSV: Complete Works of Swami Vivekananda, 2006, Kolkata: Advaita Ashram.

Feurstein, George, 2002, *The Yoga Tradition*, Delhi: Motilal Banarsidass.

Frawley, David, 2004, *Yoga and Ayurveda*, Delhi: Motilal Banarsidass.

Gandhi, M.K., 2001, *An Autobiography or The Story of My Experiments with Truth*, Ahmedabad: Navajivan Publishing House.

Gupta, Mahendranath, 2007, *The Gospel of Sri Ramakrishna*, Kolkata: Advaita Ashrama.

Hariharananda, Paramahansa, 2008, *Kriya Yoga*, New Delhi: Motilal Banarsidass.

Health and Healing in Yoga (Selections from the writings and talks of the mother), Pondicherry: Sri Aurobindo Ashram, 1998.

Iyengar, B.K.S., 1995, *The Illustrated Light on Yoga*, London: Thorsons.

——, 2000, *The Tree of Yoga*, India: HarperCollins.

Joshi, Pooran Chandra, 2001, *Sanskriti Vikas aur Sanchar Kranti*, Delhi: Grantha Shilpi.

Kalyan: Yogāṅka, 1992, Year 10, Issue 1, Gorakhpur: Gita Press.

Korpal, Nitin and Ganesh Shankar, 2005, *Hatha Yoga for Human Health*, New Delhi: Satyam Publishing House.

Krishnananda, Swami, 1990, *Essays in Life and Eternity*, Shivananda Nagar: The Divine Life Society.

Maheshananda, Swami, 2009, *Shiv Samhita*, Lonawala: Kaivalyadhama Sri Manmadhav Yoga Mandir Samiti.

Muktibodhananda, Swami, 2006, *Hatha-Yoga Pradipika*, Munger: Yoga Publication Trust.

Osborne, Arthur, 2006, *Ramana Maharshi and the Path of Self-knowledge*, Tiruvannamalai: Sri Ramanasramam.

Osho, 2002, *Yoga Moving to the Centre*, New Delhi: Fusion Books.

Pandey, Rajkumari, 1993, *Bhartiya Yoga Parampara ke Vividh Ayam*, New Delhi: Radha Publications.

Pandya, Pranav, 2009, *The Pioneers of Scientific Spirituality*, Haridwar: Sri Vedmata Gayatri Trust.

Pavitrananda, Swami, 2000, *Common Sense about Yoga*, Kolkata: Advaita Ashrama.

Ramdev, Swami, 2009, *Jeevan Darshan*, Haridwar: Divya Yoga Mandir Trust.

Saraswati, Swami Niranjanananda, 1989, *Yoga and Kriya*, Munger: Bihar School of Yoga.

——, 1997, *Gheranda Samhita*, Munger: Yoga Bharti.

——, 1998, *Rog aur Yoga*, Munger: Yoga Publications Trust.

——, 1999a, *Yoga Darshan*, Munger: Yoga Publications Trust.

——, 1999b, *Yoga Sadhana*, Munger: Bihar School of Yoga.

Saraswati, Swami Satyananda, 2001, *Bhakti Yoga Sagar*, vol. 2, Munger: Yoga Publication Trust.

——, 2002, *Asana, Pranayama, Mudra, Bandha*, Munger: Yoga Publication Trust.

——, 2003a, *Yoga Nidra*, Munger: Yoga Publication Trust.

——, 2003b, *Yoga Education for Children*, Munger: Yoga Publication Trust.

Saraswati, Swami Vijnanananda, 1998, *Yoga Vigyan*, Rishikesh: Yoga Niketan Trust.

Sardananda, Swami, 2003, *Sri Ramakrishna: The Great Master*, Kolkata: Advaita Ashrama.

Sharma, R.P., 1987, *Indian Philosophy*, Patna: Bharati Bhawan.

Shriram Sharma Acharya, 1998a, *Vangamaya: Grihastha ek Tapovana*, Mathura: Akhand Jyoti Sansthan.

——, 1998b, *Vangamaya: Mahapurushon ke Avismarniya Jivan Prasanga*, Mathura:

Akhand Jyoti Sansthan.

——, 1998c, *Vangamaya: Sadhana se Siddhi-2*, Mathura: Akhand Jyoti Sansthan.

——, 1998d, *Vangamaya: Samajik, Naitik evam Bauddhik Kranti, Kaise*? Mathura: Akhand Jyoti Sansthan.

——, 2004, *My Life: Its Legacy and Message*, Mathura: Yug Nirmana Yojana, Gayatri Tapobhumi.

——, 2010, *Bhakti Yoga,* Yoga Publication Trust.

Shivananda, Swami, 1970, *Practice of Yoga*, Shivananda Nagar: The Divine Life Society.

——, 1979, *Spiritual Experiences*, Shivananda Nagar: The Divine Life Society.

——, 1998, *From Man to God Man*, Durban: Divine Life Society.

——, 1999a, *Raja Yoga*, Shivananada Nagar: The Divine Life Society.

——, 1999b, *Tripple Yoga*, Shivananda Nagar: The Divine Life Society.

Shri Yogendra, 1978, *Yoga Essays*, Bombay: Yoga Institute.

Souvenir: Idam Yogay (International Yoga Festival 2008), Uttarakhand Tourism Development Board, Patel Nagar, Dehradun, 2008.

Souvenir: International Festival on Yoga, Culture and Spirituality, DSVV, Shantikunj, Haridwar, 2010.

Souvenir: Yoga for Health and Social Transformation, Divya Prakashan, Divya Yoga Mandir Trust, Patanjali Yogapeeth, Haridwar, 2011.

Sri Ramacharitmanas, Delhi: Motilal Banarsidass, 1996.

The Bhagvadgita, Gorakhpur: Gita Press.

Vaidik, Ved Pratap, 2002, *Hindi Patrakarita ke Vividh Ayam*, New Delhi: Hindi Book Centre.

Vivekananda, Swami, 2000, *Six Lessons on Raja-Yoga*, Calcutta: Advaita Ashrama.

——, 2001, *Bhakti Yoga*, Kolkata: Advaita Ashrama.

——, 2002, *Jnana Yoga*, Kolkata: Advaita Ashrama.

——, 2003, *Raja Yoga*, Kolkata: Advaita Ashrama.

——, 2007, *Karma Yoga*, Nagpur: Ramakrishna Math.

Yoga Darshan, Gorakhpur: Gita Press.

Yogananda, Paramahansa, 1966, *Man's Eternal Quest*, Yogada Satsang Society of India.

——, 1997, *Autobiography of a Yogi*, Mumbai: Jaico Publishing House.

Newspapers

ENGLISH

Business Standard

Economics Times

Hindu

Hindustan Times

Indian Express

Times of India

Tribune

HINDI

Amar Ujala

Dainik Jagran

Hindustan

Jansatta

Nai Duniya

Nav Bharat Times

Punjab Kesari

Rashtriya Sahara

Magazines

Aayushman, Bi-Monthly, Aayushman Corporate Office, Bhopal

Aha Jindagi, Monthly, Dainik Bhaskar Group

Akhand Jyoti, Monthly, Akhand Jyoti Sansthan, Mathura

Arogya Sanjivini, Quarterly, Pioneer Book Co.

Ayurveda-Vikas, Monthly, Dabur India, Sahibabad, Ghaziabad

Bhagvad Darshan, Monthly Bhakti Vedant Book Trust, Mumbai

Divine Life, Monthly, Divine Life Society, Shivananda Nagar, Rishikesh

Eternal Solution, Monthly, Safdarjung Enclave, New Delhi

Frontline, Weekly, Kasturi and Sons, Chennai

Health aur Nutrition, Monthly, Maigna Publishing Co, Mumbai

India News, Weekly, Good Morning India Media, New Delhi

India Today, Weekly, Living Media, New Delhi

Kadambari, Monthly, HT Media, New Delhi

Kalyan, Monthly, Gita Press, Gorakhpur

Kendra Bharati, Monthly, Advaita Ashrama, Kolkata

Kurukshetra, Monthly, Prakashan Vibhag, Suchna Bhawan, New Delhi

Life Positive, Monthly, Megas Media, New Delhi

Navnit, Monthly, Bhartiya Vidya Bhawan, Mumbai

Nirogadham, Monthly, Ajit Painters and Publishers, Indore

Nirogasukha, Bi-Monthly, Vidyadhar Nagar Publication, Jaipur

Nisargopachar, Monthly, National Institute of Naturopathy, Pune

Outlook, Monthly, Outlook Publishing, New Delhi

Prabuddha Bharat, Monthly, Advaita Ashrama, Kolkata

Rishi Prasad, Monthly, Sant Shri Asaramji Bapu Ashram, Ahmedabad

Samanvaya Sadhana Path, Monthly, Samanvaya Seva Trust, Haridwar

Sanskriti Sanchar, Half Yearly, Special Supplement, DSVU, Haridwar

Shukravar, Pearls News Network

Soham, Bi-Monthly, Nityananda International, New Delhi

Tahalaka, Anant Media, Lucknow

The Week, Weekly, Malayala Manorama, Kochi, Kerala

Uday India, Fortnightly, Sahara India Mass Comm. Press, Noida

Vatsalya Nirjhar, Monthly, Param Shaktipeeth, Lav, Indraprastha

Veda Amrita, Monthly, Pioneer Comm., Badala, Mumbai

Vivek Jyoti, Monthly, Ramakrishna Mission, Vivekananda Ashrama, Raipur

Yoga and Total Health, Monthly, Yoga Institute, Mumbai

Yoga Mimamsa, Quarterly, Kaivalyadhama, Lonavala, Pune

Yoga Patrika, Monthly, Swami Keshwananda Yoga Institute, Delhi

Yoga Sandesh, Monthly, Divya Yoga Mandir Trust, Haridwar

Yoga Sudha, Monthly, Swami Vivekananda Yoga Prakashan, Bangalore

Yoga Vidya, Monthly, Bihar School of Yoga, Munger

Yoga Vijnana, Quarterly, Morarji Desai National Institute of Yoga, New Delhi

Yoga, The Science, Monthly, Yoga Publications, Hubli, Karnataka

Yojna, Monthly, Prakashan Vibhag, Suchna Bhawan, New Delhi

Yug Nirman Yojna, Monthly, Gayatri Tapobhoomi, Mathura

Websites

www.ananda.org

www.awgp.org

www.bharatyog.com

www.disha.org/teachings/bhaktiyoga

www.hindustanwisdom.info

www.indianetzone.com

www.kamalaya.com

www.orientlia.org

www.sivananda.org

www.spiritus-temporis.com

www.wikipedia.org

www.yogapoint.com

www.yogamovement.com

www.expression of spirit.com

www.ilove India.com

www.hinduism.com

www.holisticonline.com

www.united India.com

www.vedanet.com

http://epaper.timesofIndia.com

www.pypt.org

www.answers.com

www.ehow.com

www.self-realization.com

www.medindia.net

www.indiaedu.com

yogainhighereducation.blogspot.com

www.indiadivine.org

www.wellbeing.com

www.times of India.indiatimes.com

ascentmagazine.com

www.yogamag.net

www.merinews.com

www.presscouncil.nic.in

www.mediahelpingmedia.org

www.messagefrommasters.com

allIndiamediateachers.com

www.mkgandhi.org

www.mkgandhi-sarvodaya.org

Index